Tricks and Tips

for the

C-128

By Tobias Weltner, Ralf Hornig and Jens Trapp

A Data Becker Book

Published by

Abacus Software

P.O. Box 7211
Grand Rapids, MI 49510

COMMODORE, VIC-20, C-64, C-128, 1701, and DATASETTE are trademarks (™) or registered trademarks (®) of Commodore Business Machines, Inc.

Third Printing, April 1986
Printed in U.S.A.
Copyright © 1985   Data Becker GmbH
                         Merowingerstr. 30
                         4000 Dusseldorf, West Germany
Copyright © 1985, 1986   ABACUS Software, Inc.
                         P.O. BOX 7211
                         Grand Rapids, MI. 49510

ISBN   0-916439-43-7

TABLE OF CONTENTS

FOREWARD

We've written this book for every Commodore 128 owner wanting to make better use of his or her machine. Whether you want to create your own character set, use the higher computing speed (C-128 FAST mode) in your C-64 programs, or use the ROM routines, you'll find this book full of practical information. Some of the topics covered in this book include: Banking and memory configurations; VIC-II chip registers; windows; multitasking; command extensions; important memory locations; and many, many sample programs.

We've tested and debugged all of the BASIC programs, as well as the BASIC loaders that match the machine language listings. An optional companion disk is available containing all of the programs in this book. See the ordering instructions at the end of this book for details. We used a modified version of the *LISTING CONVERTER* program (found in Chapter 3) to transfer the program listings from the C-128 to the computer with which this book was edited. There should be no errors as far as the listings themselves are concerned. The text proper will describe the operation of the programs. Before we go into the depths of the C-128, we'll just remind you of Murphy's Laws on Programming*:

1)   Once a running version of a program is ready, it's obsolete.

2)   All other programs cost more and take longer to run.

3)   If a program is useful, odds are it can be replaced.

4)   If a program is useless, it will be documented.

5)   Every completed program takes up all the memory, whether it was written that way or not.

6)   The value of a program is proportionate to the time taken in mass-producing it.

7)   Program development takes so long that by the time you get it running, you'll have to revise it to keep up with the times.

Have fun.

Tobias Weltner
Ralf Hornig
Jens Trapp

Rinteln, Germany, August 1985

* Source: A. Bloch, *"Why What Can Go Wrong, WILL"*, Goldman, 1977

CHAPTER 1

GRAPHICS ON THE COMMODORE 128

Graphics are an intriguing subject, particularly when we're talking about high-resolution graphics (as opposed to the graphic symbols built into the C-128 character set). For those who were stopped from writing professional software for the Commodore 64 because of its 40-column screen, this new machine offers another possibility. If you look on the back of the computer, you'll see two jacks marked **RF** and **VIDEO**; these allow you to connect the C-128 to a television set (RF) and a composite monitor (such as the Commodore 1701). These two jacks give you 40 columns, as with the C-64, but the 128 has one more jack -- an interface marked **RGB**! An RGB monitor (Red Green Blue) is much more expensive when compared to, say, the 1701, but with the RGB monitor you get better picture quality, higher resolution and, most importantly, an 80-column screen.

The next few pages discuss exactly what can be done with the graphics screen. Numerous sample programs illustrate these discussions. Remember that one major difference exists between the C-64 and C-128 graphics: the C-128 allows two completely independent screens, which we'll discuss next.

1.1 SWITCHING: 40/80 COLUMNS

Before going into any detail, we should take a look at switching between the 40-column and 80-column screens. The setting of the 40/80 DISPLAY key on the upper section of the keyboard determines the screen mode when powered on. After power-up, the switch is inoperative unless the reset button is pressed. To switch modes within a program use the following commands:

```
ESC+X                    (switches direct mode on)
PRINT CHR$(27)+"X"    (switches mode outside program)
SYS 49194                (works like the switching from BASIC,
                          but also works in machine language)
```

1.2 THE 40-CHARACTER SCREEN

The 40 column screen is controlled by the VIC 8564 chip. The VIC 8564 is similar to the VIC 6564 chip in the 64, but it contains an additional two registers (more on this later). When using the 40 column mode, the screen can be displayed on either a television or a composite monitor, but NOT on an RGB monitor.

Video RAM and color memory use the same memory ranges as those in the 64:

```
SCREEN RAM   $0400 - $07FF   (decimal 1024 - 2023)
COLOR  RAM   $D800 - $DBFF   (decimal 55296-56295)
```

Both ranges are in normal address space, and can be manipulated using PEEK and POKE:

```
10 FOR A=0 TO 255
20 POKE 1024+A,A
30 NEXT A
40 :
50 FOR A=0 TO 255
60 X=INT(RND(1)*16):REM RANDOM NUMBER (COLOR)
70 POKE 55296+A,X
80 NEXT A
```

The statement:

```
POKE 1024+column+(40*line),0-255
```

puts a character onto a forty-column screen; while the statement:

```
POKE 55296+column+(40*line),0-15
```

puts a color into the matching memory location. In either statement, `column` can range in value from 0 to 39 and `line` can range from 0 to 24.

As in the C-64, screen memory can be moved in 1K steps, but color memory is not relocatable.

1.3 THE 40-COLUMN CHARACTER GENERATOR

The actual design of a character is stored in a ROM known as the character generator. The character generator is found in memory at $D000 to $DFFF. You can't read the character generator by normal means, since it lies in ROM, and you can't write to it at all.

The internal divisions of the character generator look like this:

CHARACTER SET 1 (UPPER CASE and BLOCK GRAPHICS)

    $D000 - $D1FF   Upper case letters

    $D200 - $D3FF   Block characters

    $D400 - $D5FF   Reverse upper case letters

    $D600 - $D7FF   Reverse block graphics

CHARACTER SET 2 (UPPER CASE and LOWER CASE)

    $D800 - $D9FF   Lower case letters

    $DA00 - $DBFF   Upper case letters

    $DC00 - $DDFF   Lower case reversed

    $DE00 - $DFFF   Upper case reversed

The following short program allows you to read the character generator:

```
90    PRINT "{CLR HOME} PRINT THE CHARACTER
      GENERATOR ROM"
91    PRINT :   PRINT
100   REM   OUTPUT CHAR GENERATOR
120   :
130   FOR X = 0 TO 255:   REM   256 CHARACTERS
140   FOR Z = 0 TO 7:   REM   8 BYTES EACH
150   AD = 53248 + X * 8 + Z
180   BANK 14: C =   PEEK (AD) : BANK 15
210   :
220   FOR Y = 7 TO 0 STEP   - 1:   REM   8 PIXELS/BYTE
230   IF C >   = 2 ^ Y THEN C = C - 2 ^ Y:
      PRINT "*";:   ELSE   PRINT ".";
240   NEXT Y
250   :
260   PRINT
270   NEXT Z
280   PRINT
290   NEXT X
300   END
```

The pattern of each character is stored in eight bytes; each byte is divided into eight bits. So, one character has a matrix of 64 bits. Each of these bits can be turned on or off. The character generator is taken directly from ROM in 40-column mode. Therefore to make any changes to a character's pattern, we have to copy the character generator into RAM. The ROM character generator cannot be moved or changed, but the copied generator can be moved to a different memory location.

We'll begin from a cold start in BASIC. Type the following in direct mode:

```
POKE 56,48:POKE 58*256,0:NEW
```

Any program currently in memory will be lost. To copy the character set from the character generator to RAM, use the following:

```
10  REM COPY CHARGEN $D000 TO $2000
20  BANK 14 : REM READ OUT CHARGEN
30  FOR X=0 TO 4095
40  POKE DEC("2000")+X,PEEK(DEC("D000")+X)
50  NEXT X
60  BANK 15 : REM NORMAL CONFIG.
```

Here's where we see how slow BASIC is; the entire procedure takes more than a minute! The program moves the character generator from ROM to the RAM area near the start of BASIC.

Now the character generator is in RAM. We know this, but the computer doesn't; you'll have to tell the computer to use the copied character set (64 fans will note that the address 53272 is the same). The memory contents of this location determines the starting addresses of the character generator and screen RAM. We'll skip the latter for the moment, and have a look at the character generator itself. Here's an overview of possible starting combinations:

```
SCREEN MEMORY                          CHARACTER SET
-----------------------------------    ---------------------------
0000xxxx       0                       xxxx000x        0
0001xxxx     1024                       xxxx001x     2048
0010xxxx     2048                       xxxx010x     4096
0011xxxx     3072                       xxxx011x     6144
0100xxxx     4096                       xxxx100x     8192
0101xxxx     5120                       xxxx101x    10240
0110xxxx     6144                       xxxx110x    12288
0111xxxx     7168                       xxxx111x    14336
1000xxxx     8192
1001xxxx     9216
1010xxxx    10240
1011xxxx    11264
1100xxxx    12288
1101xxxx    13312
1110xxxx    14336
1111xxxx    15360
```

The character set can be moved in 2K increments. This has two disadvantages: First, the character set can only be moved within the first 16K of memory. Second, the normal ROM character set is located at 6144, but that's normal BASIC RAM. How can that be?

The VIC chip can only address 16K, which in this case is the first 16K of memory. The address 6144 represents the offset within this 16K block. We can determine which 16K block is involved by changing the contents of address 56576:

16K range:

```
-----------------  -------------------------------------------
$0000 - $3FFF          0 - 16383    POKE 56576,199
$4000 - $7FFF      16384 - 32767    POKE 56576,198
$8000 - $BFFF      32768 - 49151    POKE 56576,197
$C000 - $FFFF      49152 - 65535    POKE 56576,196
-----------------------------------------------------------
```

When the last 16K block ($C000-$FFFF) is used (default), the character generator resides at 49152 + 4096 = 53248 ($D000). If you check the first table, you'll see that the normal character set (upper case/graphics) begins at $D000. The first two bits in 56576 represent address bits 14 and 15 of the character generator.

Keep in mind that the screen memory is also moved in 16K steps. The high byte of screen RAM has to be moved:

```
POKE 2619,4+X*64
```

```
X=0-3  (matches 16 banks 0-3)
```

To let the computer know that the new character set is at $2000, you'll have to change the contents of 53272; here we find a substantial difference between the C-128 and the C-64. Where the C-64 required only a simple POKE, here we don't have that luxury -- what you POKE will be reset by the C-128 operating system. So, to get around this, we'll have to deal with a byte in zero-page memory:

```
$0A2C(2604) VIC TEXT SCREEN/CHAR BASE POINTER
```

This looks more complicated than it actually is. POKEing into 53272 on the C-64 is equivalent to POKEing into 2604 on the C-128. The contents of this address automatically writes to 53272.

Switching to our new character set can be accomplished with this statement:

```
POKE 2604,PEEK(2604) AND NOT 2+4+8 OR 8
```

In other words, bits 1 to 3 (controlling the position of the character generator) are cleared, and bit 3 is set. So, address 53272 gives us these contents: xxxx100x

This statement sets the new character generator at 8192. Bear in mind that all we've done is move the character set around; the procedure isn't finished. Notice how odd the characters look on the screen.

1.3.1 CHANGING THE CHARACTER SET

Now, type in the following BASIC program:

```
10  REM @   SIGN TO SQUARE
20  FOR X = 0 TO 7: REM 8 BYTES PER CHARACTER
30  READ CO
40  POKE 8192+0*8+X,CO
50  NEXT X
60  DATA 255,129,129,129,129,129,129,255
```

The @ sign changes before our eyes to a square (see "Defining your Own Characters" in the 80-column section for more information).

1.3.2 40-COLUMN CHARACTER EDITOR

Fortunately, you don't need to design your new 40-column character set by hand: With a few small changes, you can use the 80-column character editor (Chapter 1.16.1). First move the start of BASIC to protect your character set from overwriting your BASIC program. In direct mode, enter:

```
POKE 46,58:POKE14848,0:NEW
```

Then change the following lines of the 80-column character editor:

```
4000  BANK 14
4010  FOR X = 0 TO 4096
4020  POKE DEC("2000")+X,PEEK(DEC("D000")=X)
4030  NEXT X
4050  POKE 2619,4
```

```
4060 POKE 56576,199
4070 POKE 2604,PEEK(2604) AND NOT 2+4+8 OR 8
4080 BANK 15
5005 - 5046 :  DELETE
5065 AD=8192+8*A+Y
5070 POKE AD,W
5075          :  DELETE
```

Edit the characters, then exit the program and RUN 4000 to enable your custom character set.

1.4 MOVING SCREEN MEMORY

Screen memory normally resides in $0400 - $07FF (1024 - 2023), but it can be relocated. Remember these two addresses:


```
2604 VIC TEXT SCREEN/CHAR BASE POINTER
2619 VIC TEXT SCREEN BASE
```

We can move screen memory anywhere in memory, in 1K steps. See Chapter 1.3 for the table showing possible addresses. Meanwhile, let's get started on uses for relocating screen memory.

1.4.1 WORKING WITH SEVERAL SCREENS

As the title suggests, you have the option of using several screens at once (called "page-flipping") in 40-column mode. We'll illustrate this using three screens. Since these three screens will use part of normal BASIC memory, you must move the start of BASIC so that your programs don't overwrite the new screen memory. In direct mode, enter the following statements:

```
POKE 46,40: POKE10240,0: NEW
```

The following BASIC program POKEs a machine language program into memory which can be used to "page flip" between three screens by using the <F1>, <F3>, and <F5> keys.

```
2000 FOR X = 4864 TO 4950
2010 READ A : CS=CS+A: POKE X,A
2020 NEXT X
2030 IF CS <> 7857 THEN PRINT CHR$(7); LIST
2040 DATA  120,169,24,141,20,3,169,19,141,21,3,
          169,0,141,0,16
2050 DATA 141,2,16,141,4,16,88,96,72,138,72,
          166,213,224,4,208
2060 DATA 13,169,20,141,44,10,169,4,141,59,
          10,76,80,19,224,5
2070 DATA 208,13,169,132,141,44,10,169,32,
          141,59,10,76,80,19,224
2080 DATA 6,208,13,169,148,141,44,10,169,
          36,141,59,10,76,80,19
2090 DATA 104,170,104,76,101,250,255
```

Here's a listing of the machine language program that is POKEd into memory by the above BASIC program:

```
1300 78          SEI            :interrupt off
1301 A9 18       LDA #$18       :low-byte of new IRQ
1303 8D 14 03    STA $0314      :store low-byte
1306 A9 13       LDA #$13       :high-byte of new IRQ
1308 8D 15 03    STA $0315      :store it
130B A9 00       LDA #$00       :Length of function keys
130D 8D 00 10    STA $1000      :F1 on
1310 8D 02 10    STA $1002      :F3 on
1313 8D 04 10    STA $1004      :F5 on
1316 58          CLI            :interrupt again permitted
1317 60          RTS            :back to BASIC
```

NEW IRQ:

```
1318 48          PHA            :put accu
1319 8A          TXA            :and X-reg
131A 48          PHA            :on stack
131B A6 D5       LDX $D5        :load X w/ pressed key
131D E0 04       CPX #$04       :F1?
131F D0 0D       BNE $132E      :no, then read next
1321 A9 14       LDA #$14       :new starting address
1323 8D 2C 0A    STA $0A2C      :and set
1326 A9 04       LDA #$04       :new screen at $0400
1328 8D 3B 0A    STA $0A3B      :and set it
132B 4C 50 1A    JMP $1350      :end F1
132E E0 05       CPX #$05       :F3?
1330 D0 0D       BNE $133F      :no, then read next
1332 A9 84       LDA #$84       :new starting address
1334 8D 2C 0A    STA $0A2C      :and set
1337 A9 20       LDA #$20       :new screen at $2000
1339 8D 3B 0A    STA #$0A3B     :and set
133C 4C 50 1A    JMP $1350      :end F3
133F E0 06       CPX #$06       :F5?
1341 D0 0D       BNE $1350      :no, then ready
1343 A9 94       LDA #$94       :new starting address
1345 8D 2C 0A    STA #$0A2C     :and set
1348 A9 24       LDA #$24       :new screen at $2400
134A 8D 3B 0A    STA $0A3B      :and set
134D 4C 50 1A    JMP $1350      :end F5
1350 68          PLA            :Put back old
1351 AA          TAX            :X-reg and
1352 68          PLA            :accumulator values,
1353 4C 65 FA    JMP $FA65      :and return normal IRQ
```

The principle is the same for 80-column mode (see Chapter 1.17).

After RUNning the program, you have your choice of three independent screen pages, called by <F1>, <F3> and <F5>. These screens will initially be full of strange characters—clear the individual screens with:

```
PRINT CHR$(147) (or with PRINT"{CLR/HOME}")
```

You can switch screens in program mode with a POKE to address 213:

```
POKE 213,4  (normal screen)
POKE 213,5  (2nd screen at $2000)
POKE 213,6  (3rd screen at $2400)
```

Here is the memory configuration used by the routine:

	SCR 1(normal)	SCR 2	SCR 3
Start of screen memory	$0400	$2000	$2400
End of screen memory	$07FF	$23FF	$27FF
Color RAM -- start	$D800	$D800	$D800
Color RAM -- end	$DBFF	$DBFF	$DBFF
BASIC start	$2800	$2800	$2800
Press	F1	F3	F5

1.5 THE 80-COLUMN SCREEN

The C-128 isn't just for games. To make it a more practical machine, it has 80-column capability, thanks to a special graphic processor called the VDC 8563 (Video Display Controller). We should mention that this chip displays 80 columns only on a RGB monitor. We'll talk about that later.

1.6. SCREEN AND COLOR RAM

Now we enter completely new territory. Screen and color RAM for 40-column mode is in normal RAM, and can be controlled by PEEKing and POKEing. But 80-column video RAM is outside of normal RAM, and can't be changed using normal PEEKs and POKEs! Don't panic yet—the next couple of pages show how we can gain control of 80-column video controller. On the next page is a list of registers for the 80-column controller. We'll cover each register in detail.

1.7 REGISTERS OF THE 80-COLUMN CONTROLLER

```
00 READ:   Status, LP,VBlank,-,-,-,-,-
   WRITE: Bits 0-5 of desired register
01 Characters per line
02 Shift screen window (horizontal/character-wise)
03 Shift screen window (horizontal/pixel-wise)
04 Vertical synchronization
05 Vertical total
06 Lines per screen page
07 Shift screen window (vertical/line-wise)
08 Interface mode
09 Matrix register -- vertical
10 Cursor mode -- begin scan
11 End scan
12 Screen memory start address -- HI
13 LO of 12
14 Cursor position -- HI
15 LO of 14
16 Light pen vertical
17 Light pen horizontal
18 Channel address HI
19 LO of 18
20 Addribute-RAM start address -- HI
21 LO of 20
22 Matrix register/display horizontal
23 Matrix display vertical
24 Smooth-scroll vertical
25 Smooth-scroll horizontal
26 Color
27 Address shifting
28 Character generator basic address -- HI
29 Underline-Cursor-Scan-Line
30 Repeat register
31 Channel, byte read/write in video RAM
32 Block start address -- HI
33 LO of 32
34 Start of screen representation
35 End of screen representation
36 refresh-rate
```

1.8 THE VIDEO DISPLAY CONTROLLER (VDC)

We'll now cover the functions of the individual registers using examples.

These registers are indirectly addressed. That means that only registers 0 and 1 can be accessed. If you want to see the contents of register 26, you'd type this in:

```
A=DEC("D600")
POKE A,26:PRINT PEEK(A+1)
```

The register number is written into register 0 ($D600); register 1 ($D601) acts as the channel for writing to or reading from the desired register:

```
10  INPUT"REGISTER";R
20  INPUT"VALUE";V
30  POKE DEC("D600"),R
40  POKE DEC("D601),V
```

Access to the Video RAM

As already mentioned, the VDC video has 16K of RAM outside of the normal address range. To access the VDC video RAM, use the following method:

```
10   BA = DEC("D600")
110  INPUT "ADDRESS OF THE VIDEO RAM";V
120  INPUT "VALUE";W
130  HO = INT(V/256): LO= V-(256*HI)
140  POKE BA, 18: POKE BA+1, HI
150  POKE BA, 19: POKE BA+1, LO
160  POKE BA, 31: POKE BA+1, W
```

```
170 WAIT BA, 32
180 POKE BA, 30: POKE BA+1, 1
```

Program explanation:

100	Store the base address of the VDC in BA
110	Prompt for desired video RAM address (V)
120	Prompt for value you want written into video RAM (W)
130	Separate V into low and high bytes
140	Put high byte desired address into register 18
150	Put low byte into register 19
160	Byte value into register 31
170	Wait command until we reach memory address BA
180	Register 30 filled with 1 (character output)

Here is the video RAM layout on power-up:

$0000 - $07FF Screen refresh memory (SCR-RAM)
(dec. 0-2047)

$0800 - $0FFF Attribute RAM (e.g. color memory)
(dec. 2048-4095)

$1000 - $1FFF free
(dec. 4096 - 8191)

$2000 - $3FFF character generator
(dec. 8192-16385)

Now we'll try to write to video RAM. Start the above BASIC program and input 0 as the desired address; then enter a value between 0 and 255. A character should appear in the upper left-hand corner of the 80-column screen -- the character displayed depends upon the value you enter.

To tell you the truth, this method of accessing video RAM is pretty unreliable, but you can repeatedly write to this RAM (as long as it's within bounds!). On the other hand, this isn't a method for a serious programmer. We'll give you another method in the next section.

1.9 PRACTICAL VIDEO RAM ACCESS

What does the operating system do when a key is pressed while in 80-column mode? It seems to work perfectly. Well, let's explore how the operating system treats characters in this mode. Of particular interest is a ROM routine which you can easily call yourself. Here it is:

```
SYS 49155,CHARACTER,COLOR


     CHARACTER     =char #(0-255)
     COLOR         =char. color (0-16)
```

Unlike the previous BASIC routine, this routine always works. Plus, this routine works for both the 40- and 80-column screens. This means that it's possible to program for both screens at once (or two separate monitors).

Once the novelty of the above routine wears off, you may wonder how to put these characters on different lines of the screen. The position of the character is read from memory locations 224 and 225 (current cursor position). If you want a character in a specific place, you'll have to play around a bit with these memory locations:

```
10 AD = CLMN + PEEK(238)* LINE
20 S1 = PEEK (224): S2 = PEEK(225)
30 HI = (AD/256): LO = AD-(256*HI)
40 POKE 244, LO: POKE 225, HI
50 SYS 49155, CHARACTER, COLOR
60 POKE 224, S1: POKE 225, S2
70 END
```

CLMN:0-79 (0-39)
LINE :0-24

238	Maximum length of screen
224	Cursor position -- LOW
225	Cursor position -- HIGH
49155	Start address -- ROM routine

1.10 POKE SIMULATION

This machine language routine does away with all the compromises of the previous techniques; we call it a "modified POKE command". Basically, it's a pseudo-POKE for 80-column video RAM.

```
1800 48        PHA        :Get char from stack
1801 8A        TXA        :low byte address
1802 48        PHA        :placed on stack
1803 98        TYA        :high byte address
1804 48        PHA        :put on stack
1805 A9 02     LDA #$02
```

```
1807 8D 28 0A STA $0A28   :set cursor flag
180A A2 12    LDX #$12    :VDC register 18
180C 68       PLA         :get high byte back
180D 20 1B 1C JSR $181B   :set register
1810 E8       INX         :VDC register 19
1811 68       PLA         :get back low byte
1812 20 1B 1C JSR $181B   :set register
1815 A2 1F    LDX #$1F    :VDC register 31
1817 68       PLA         :get back character
1818 4C 1B 1C JMP $181B   :set register -- ready
-------------------------------------------------
181B 8E 00 D6 STX $D600   :register 0
181E 2C 00 D6 BIT $D600   :bit 7 set?
1821 10 FB    BPL $1C8E   :no -- then test again
1823 8D 01 D6 STA $D601   :give value in D601
1826 60       RTS
```

For those of you who don't program in machine language, here is the
BASIC loader.

```
5    REM  1.10A
10   FOR X = 6144 TO 6182
20   READ A: CS = CS + A:  POKE X,A
30   NEXT X
40   IF CS <  > 3411 THEN  PRINT  CHR$ (7);:  LIST
50   DATA 72,138,72,152,72,169,2,141,40,10,162,18
60   DATA 104,32,27,24,232,104,32,27,24,162,31,104
70   DATA 76,27,24,142,0,214,44,0,214,16,251,141
80   DATA 1,214,96
```

Now you have an extended POKE command at your disposal, which uses
the following format:

```
SYS DEC ("1800"),CHR,LO,HI
```

```
CHR    = character/byte-value (0-255)
LO     = low byte of desired address
HI     = high byte of desired address
```

Try this:

```
10 INPUT "ADDRESS";AD
20 HI=INT(AD/256):LO=AD-(256*HI)
30 SYS DEC("1800"),3,LO,HI
```

Given an address of 0; immediately a "C" (3 = screen code C) appears at the HOME area of the 80-column screen. Restart the routine, and input a value of 2048 -- now the "C" is in cyan; you've written it to *attribute* RAM (2048-3047).

One byte of attribute RAM is configured as follows:

```
BIT 0   brightness
BIT 1   blue
BIT 2   green
BIT 3   red
BIT 4   blink
BIT 5   underline
BIT 6   reverse video
BIT 7   2nd character set
```

The use of the first four bits is obvious: combining these bits results in the 16 available colors. Setting bit 4 causes the corresponding character to blink rapidly.

Just for fun, put this new line into the program we just typed in:

```
30 SYS DEC("1800"),2^0+2^3+2^4,LO,HI
```

Now when you input 2048 for AD, the first character on screen blinks pink (light red)! You can also put characters into reverse video or underscore them by setting bit 6 or bit 5 (respectively). Bit 7 lets you change character sets, just as <SHIFT/C=> does. On the 80-column screen it's possible to have BOTH character sets onscreen at the same time, unlike in 40-column mode. This means that you have 512 characters to work with!

1.11 THE CHARACTER GENERATOR

Having 512 characters at your fingertips may seem like a lot, but for special purposes (games, math characters, special alphabets, etc.), the in-house character set just isn't enough. So, you have to go in and design the missing characters on your own. This is somewhat easier to do in 80-column mode, since the character generator is already in RAM, and can be changed from there without having to copy it from ROM or moving the start of BASIC.

1.12 READING THE CHARACTER GENERATOR

Now we'll read out the character generator from video RAM:

```
20      BA = 8192
30      A =  DEC ("D600"): B = A + 1
40      FOR X = 0 TO 7
50      AD = BA + X + 8 * W:  IF AD > 16383 THEN  END
60      HI =  INT (AD / 256): LO = AD - (256 * HI)
70      POKE A,18:  POKE B,HI
80      POKE A,19:  POKE B,LO
90      POKE A,31: CH =  PEEK (B)
100      FOR Y = 7 TO 0 STEP  - 1
110      IF CH >  = 2 ^ Y THEN CH = CH - 2 ^ Y:
         PRINT "*";:  ELSE  PRINT ".";
120      NEXT Y
130      PRINT
140      NEXT X
150      W = W + 1
160      GOTO 40
```

Variables used:

BA	:Base of character generator
A	:Base of VDC
AD	:Current address in character generator
HI	:High byte of AD
LO	:Low byte of AD
CH	:Read-out value of character line
W	:Counter

RUNning the program causes all the characters to be displayed in an enlarged matrix on the screen. You'll note that eight spaces follow every character. Also note that the 80-column character generator of the C-128 is quite different from those of the VIC-20, or even the C-64.

You see, every character is made up of 16 bytes, as opposed to the eight bytes of the VIC or 64. Contrary to the way it sounds, there is no waste here; normal circumstances give eight bytes per character unused. These "empty bytes" serve a specific purpose -- the VDC 8563 can produce character matrices in either 8 X 8 or 16 X 8 format; see the figure below.

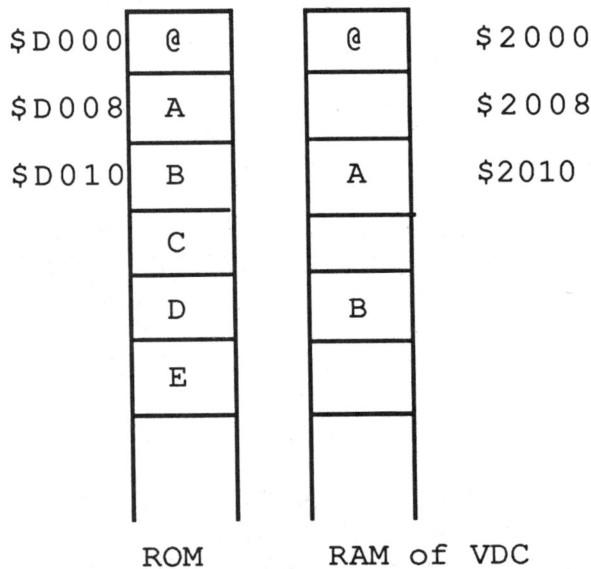

1.13 BIG SCRIPT WITH STRINGS

Here is another useful program using the Character Generator. There's
nothing stopping us from making enlarged characters. Try this program.

```
10       Z$ = "*":  GOSUB 60000:  PRINT Z$:  END
60000    Z =  ASC (Z$): Z$ = "":  IF Z AND 128
         THEN X = Z AND 127 OR 64:  GOTO 60040
60010    IF  NOT Z AND 64 THEN X = Z:  GOTO 60040
60020    IF Z AND 32 THEN X = Z AND 95:  GOTO 60040
60030    X = Z AND 63
60040    L$ = "": U$ = ""
60050    FOR W = 0 TO 7
60060    L$ = L$ +  CHR$ (157)
60070    U$ = U$ +  CHR$ (145)
60080    NEXT W
60090    D$ =  CHR$ (17)
60100    REM   CHARACTER GENERATOR SELECTION
60110    A =  DEC ("D600"): B = A + 1
60120    :
60130    FOR Z = 0 TO 7:  REM  8 BYTES
60140    AD = 8192 + X * 16 + Z
60150    HI =  INT (AD / 256): LO = AD - (256 * HI)
60160    :
60170    POKE A,18:  POKE B,HI
60180    POKE A,19:  POKE B,LO
60190    POKE A,31: C =  PEEK (B)
60200    :
60210    FOR Y = 7 TO 0 STEP  - 1:  REM  8 PIXEL
         LINES/CHARACTER
60220    IF C >  = 2 ^ Y THEN C = C - 2 ^ Y: ZE$ =
         ZE$ + "*":ELSE ZE$ = ZE$ + "{SPACE}"
60230    NEXT Y
60240    Z$ = Z$ + ZE$ + L$ + D$: ZE$ = ""
60250    NEXT Z
60260    Z$ =  LEFT$ (Z$, LEN (Z$) - 9) + U$
60270    RETURN
```

1.14 PRINTING BANNERS AT HOME

Now that we have enlarged characters on the screen, we might as well print them to the printer. This program will let you print banners and posters of any length. You have a choice of sizes from 8 to 80 times larger than normal:

```
10   S$ = "*": L$ = " "
20   REM  BANNER-PRINTER
30   :
40   PRINT "{CLR HOME}{RVS ON} BANNER-PRINTER {RVS
     OFF}"
50   PRINT "{CRSR DOWN}{CRSR DOWN}THIS PROGRAM
     DEMONSTRATES THE "
60   PRINT "{CRSR DOWN}USE OF THE PRINTER FOR
     VERTICAL PRINTING"
70   PRINT "{CRSR DOWN}{CRSR DOWN}TO PRINT A
     LETTER,"
80   PRINT "{CRSR DOWN}TYPE IN SIZE AND THEN HIT
     'RETURN' ."
85   PRINT :  PRINT  TAB( 7)"{CRSR DOWN}{CRSR
     DOWN}{CRSR DOWN}HIT ANY KEY TO CONTINUE"
90   GET  KEY A$
100 OPEN 4,4
110 PRINT "{CLR HOME}{RVS ON} SIDEWAYS-PRINTER
     {RVS OFF}"
120 PRINT "{CRSR DOWN}{CRSR DOWN}  ENTER SIZE:
     {CRSR DOWN}{CRSR DOWN}"
130 INPUT "{CRSR DOWN}{CRSR DOWN}HEIGHT (1-10)
     ";HO
140 INPUT "WIDTH  (1-...)";BR
150 PRINT "AT COLON-TYPE LETTER TO PRINT"
155 PRINT "HIT [RETURN] TO STOP"
160 PRINT ": ";:  POKE 208,0: GET KEY A$:PRINT A$;
165 IF A$ =  CHR$ (13) THEN  END
170 :
180 AC =  ASC (A$)
190 IF AC AND 128 THEN CO = AC AND 127 OR 64:
     GOTO 230
```

```
200 IF   NOT AC AND 64 THEN CO = AC:   GOTO 230
210 IF AC AND 32 THEN CO = AC AND 95:   GOTO 230
220 CO = AC AND 63
230 REM   ** CHAR CODES   **
240 BANK 14
250 FOR A = 0 TO 7
260 CH(A) =   PEEK (53248 + (8 * CO) + A)
270 NEXT A
280 BANK 15
290 :
300 REM   ** CHAR ROTATE **
310 FOR A = 0 TO 7
320 K(A) = 0
330 NEXT A
340 FOR A = 0 TO 7
350 FOR B = 7 TO 0 STEP  - 1
360 W = 2 ^ B
370 IF CH(A) >= W THEN CH(A) = CH(A) - W: K(7 -
    B) = K(7 - B) + 2 ^ A
380 NEXT B,A
390 :
400 REM   ** CHAR OUTPUT **
410 FOR I = 0 TO 7
420 Q$ = ""
430 FOR J = 7 TO 0 STEP  - 1
440 WI = K(I) AND 2 ^ J
450 IF WI THEN   FOR U = 1 TO HO: Q$ = Q$ + S$:
    NEXT U:   GOTO 470
460 FOR U = 1 TO HO: Q$ = Q$ + L$:   NEXT U
470 NEXT J
480 REM   ** DELETE UNNECESSARY BEGINNING SPACES **
490 LX =   LEN (Q$) - 1
500 IF   RIGHT$ (Q$,1) = " " THEN Q$ =   LEFT$
    (Q$,LX):   GOTO 490
510 FOR U = 1 TO BR
520 PRINT# 4,Q$
530 NEXT U
540 NEXT I
550 GOTO 160
```

1.15 DEFINING YOUR OWN CHARACTER SETS

Now we'll redefine the built-in character set using our pseudo POKE program from Chapter 1.10. To help you, we've supplied the following program.

Normally, every character is built within an 8 X 8 matrix. A good monitor will allow you to see these individual points. The "A" character looks like this when enlarged:

```
76543210
...**...0
..****..1
.**..**.2
.******.3
.**..**.4
.**..**.5
.**..**.6
........7
```

This is what you get when you run the character generator reading program. You have this same matrix in which to design each of your own characters (if you want still more, read on). Every line of a character consumes one byte of memory, and each pixel within a byte is equal to one bit. Each bit shows a point when it is set (1).

RUN the following program, which turns the "@" sign into a square:

```
10 A = DEC("D600"): B= A+1
20 BA = 8192: ZE= 0
30 FOR X = 0 TO 7
40 AD = BA + X + (8*ZE)
50 HI = INT(AD/256) : LO = AD - (HI*256)
```

```
60 READ CH
70 SYS ("DEC1800"),CH,LO,HI
80 NEXT X
90 END
100 DATA 255,129,129,129,129,129,129,255
```

Now for an explanation of what happens:

10   A=base if VDC, B=register 1

20   BA=base of char. generator, ZE= character to be altered
      (A=1, B=2, etc.)

30   change 8 bytes

40   byte address=base of char. gen+byte number+8*char. number

50   AD converted into low byte/high byte format

60   read new byte values

70   modified POKE routine POKEs value into video RAM

100   DATA for square:

```
76543210
********0 255 (2^7+2^6+2^5+2^4+2^3+2^2+2^1+2^0)
*......*1 129 (2^7+2^0)
*......*2 129 (2^7+2^0)
*......*3 129 (2^7+2^0)
*......*4 129 (2^7+2^0)
*......*5 129 (2^7+2^0)
*......*6 129 (2^7+2^0)
********7 255 (2^7+2^6+2^5+2^4+2^3+2^2+2^1+2^0)
```

Now, change line 100 to this

```
100 DATA 60,66,157,161,161,157,66,60
```

or this:

```
100 DATA 66,157,161,161,161,161,157,66
```

and press the "@" key.

1.16 80-COLUMN CHARACTER EDITOR

You could redefine the entire character set by hand, and POKE it into memory. You don't need to, though; use this program instead.

```
1       ZN = 5100
2       MA = 7
3       DIM D(MA),W$(MA)
10      D$ = "........"
20      REM  CHARACTER-EDITOR (80-COLUMN-CHARSET)
30      FOR Y = 0 TO 7: D(Y) = 0:   NEXT Y
31      PRINT "{CLR HOME}{RVS ON}{WHT}80-COLUMN
        CHARSET EDITOR-EDIT CHARACTER {RVS OFF}"
32      MF = 1
40      PRINT
50      PRINT "ENTER CHARACTER TO EDIT,    -->";
        :  GET  KEY C$
55      PRINT C$:  PRINT : PRINT
60      AC =  ASC (C$)
70      IF AC AND 128 THEN CO = AC AND 127:  GOTO 110
80      IF  NOT AC AND 64 THEN CO = AC:  GOTO 110
90      IF AC AND 32 THEN CO = AC AND 95:   GOTO 110
100     CO = AC AND 63
110     AD = 53248 + CO * 8
120     C$ = ""
130     :
140      PRINT "{CRSR DOWN}{RVS ON}{GRN} ORIGINAL
         {RVS OFF}          {RVS ON}{L GRN}    USER
         {RVS OFF}"
150      BANK 14
160      FOR X = 0 TO MA
170      CZ =  PEEK (AD + X):   IF X > 7 THEN CZ = 0
180      FOR Y = 7 TO 0 STEP  - 1
190      IF CZ >  = 2 ^ Y THEN C$ = C$ +"{WHT}*{GRN}'
         : CZ = CZ - 2 ^ Y:  ELSE C$ = C$ + "."
200      NEXT Y
210      PRINT "{GRN}";C$;X; TAB( 16);"{L GRN}";:
         PRINT  USING "##";X;
211      PRINT  TAB( 19);D$
```

```
220     C$ = ""
230     NEXT X
231     PRINT "{RVS ON}{GRN}               {RVS OFF}
        {RVS ON}{L GRN}            {RVS OFF}"
232     BANK 15
240     :
260     REM  EDITOR-ROUTINE
270     PRINT "{WHT}";
271     OPEN 1,0
280     FOR Y = 0 TO MA
290     CHAR ,16,7 + Y
300     PRINT " ->";
301     WINDOW 19,7 + Y,27,7 + Y,MF
302     POKE 244,1:   INPUT# 1,W$(Y)
310     W$(Y) = LEFT$ (W$(Y),8)
311     WINDOW 0,0,79,24:   REM  0,0,39,24 FOR 40
        COLUMN
320     FOR X = 1 TO 8
330     IF  MID$ (W$(Y),X,1) = "*" THEN D(Y) = D(Y)
        + 2 ^ (8 - X)
340     NEXT X
350     NEXT Y
351     CLOSE 1
360     CHAR ,0,22:   PRINT "CORRECTIONS (Y/N) ?";:
        GET  KEY A$
370     IF A$ = "Y" THEN MF = 0:   FOR Y = 0 TO 7:
        D(Y) = 0:   NEXT Y:   GOTO 260
380     PRINT :   PRINT "USE CHARACTER (Y/N) ?";:
        GET  KEY A$
390     IF A$ = "N" THEN 30
400     REM  USE CHARACTER
1000    PRINT "{CLR HOME}{CRSR DOWN}{CRSR DOWN}";
1010    ZN = ZN + 10
1020    PRINT ZN;"DATA ";CO;",";
1030    FOR X = 0 TO MA:   PRINT D(X);"{CRSR
        LEFT},";:   NEXT X
1031    PRINT "{CRSR LEFT} "
1032    PRINT ZN + 10;"DATA -1"
1039    PRINT :   PRINT "GOTO 30"
1040    PRINT "{HOME}";
1050    FOR Y = 842 TO 845:   POKE Y,13:   NEXT Y
1060    POKE 208,4
1070    END
```

```
5000    REM   BASIC-LOADER CHARACTER DEFINITION
5005    FOR X = 6144 TO 6182
5010    READ A
5015    CS = CS + A
5020    POKE X,A
5025    NEXT X
5030    IF CS < > 3411 THEN  PRINT  CHR$ (7):  LIST
        5035 - 5050:  END
5035    DATA 72,138,72,152,72,169,2,141,40,10,162,18
5040    DATA 104,32,27,24,232,104,32,27,24,162,31
5045    DATA 104,76,27,24,142,0,214,44,0,214,16,251
5046    DATA 141,1,214,96
5050    READ A:  IF A =  - 1 THEN  END
5055    FOR Y = 0 TO 7
5060    READ W
5065    AD = 8192 + 16 * A + Y
5070    HI =  INT (AD / 256): LO = AD - (256 * HI)
5075    SYS  DEC ("1800"),W,LO,HI
5080    NEXT Y
5085    GOTO 5050
```

Variables:

ZN:	first line number of DATA statements
MA:	matrix 8*MA+1
D(x):	DATA used to calculate character
W$(x):	given character line
C$:	character to be changed
AC:	ASCII code of C$
CO:	screen code of ASCII character
CZ:	read-out ROM data
CS:	checksum

Program description:

Don't let the size of this program throw you off; for a well-equipped character editor, it's really a very short program! Be sure to SAVE the program before running it.

Once started, the generator will ask for the first character that you want changed; just press the desired key. Two 8 X 8 character matrices will appear; the left matrix will contain the original character, while the right matrix is for you to do your "paperwork". Asterisks ("*") represent set points, and periods (".") stand for no point.

When you've finished modifying each line, press the <RETURN> key. Once the character is done, you have the option of going in to make corrections. If you wish to do so, press "Y", and make your corrections. If everything is right, just press <RETURN>.

Assuming that the finished character is to your satisfaction, the character editor figures out the DATA statements for you. Once all the characters are changed, stop the program with the <RUN/STOP> key, and type in:

```
DELETE -5000.
```

The editor/generator is deleted, leaving you with a BASIC loader starting at line 5000 (you might want to change the numbering now, using the RENUMBER command). This loader goes into your program, changing only the characters you wished to change -- the other characters appear as normal.

50 - 120   Commodore-specific screen code is stored in C$ (very different from the ASCII code).

140 - 232   Screen mask is designed. The memory configuration is switched with BANK 14, by which the ROM character set at $D000 can be read. Finally, a character is read out bit-by-bit, and the bits are set. After reading ROM, configuration switches back to BANK 15.

260 - 351   Editor routine: Screen is opened for data, using INPUT without question mark. Every input line of the user matrix is defined in a window.

360 - 400   Prompts: Any corrections? If so, MF will be set to 0, the window will remain uncleared. D(Y) will be cleared.

1000 - 1039   DATA line of the last character will be printed out in CHAR. CODE, NUMBERS format. Last DATA statement will be -1.

1040 - 1070   Keyboard buffer fills with <RETURN>s, and line is rewritten. For more information on how this works, see Chapter 5.

5000 - 5085   Start of the BASIC loader being produced, with the modified POKE implemented in lines 5005-5045. This section also contains a read loop for the character DATA still to be added.

1.17 WORKING WITH MULTIPLE SCREENS

Video RAM layout:

$0000 - $07FF	screen RAM (dec. 0 - 2047)
$0800 - $0FFF	color RAM, etc. (dec. 2048 - 4095)
$1000 - $1FFF	free (4096 - 8191)
$2000 - $3FFF	character generator (8192 - 16385)

Notice the memory from $1000 to $1FFF. This 4K in the middle of video RAM is unused. You can make good use of this area -- 4K is equal to 2*2K, and you can see that the screen memory ($0000-$07FF) is 2K in size. This free area gives us space to store two additional screen "pages" in addition to normal one displayed on the monitor. There are a number of uses for this. For example, you can have an invisible screen on which graphics are drawn, while you work on the visible screen, and flip back and forth between screens. Or, one screen can have a program listing, the second a disk directory, and the third the program run of the listing on the first screen.

Implementation:

The screen memory is normally found at $0000 in video RAM, but this isn't a hard and fast rule. Registers 12 and 13 of the VDC contain the high and low byte of screen memory's starting address. Three addresses must be changed to move screen memory:

VDC register 12:	high byte of the new starting address
VDC register 13:	low byte of the new starting address

Address 2606($0A2E):   high byte - new starting address

Let's say we want to move the start of screen memory from $0000 to $1000. The high byte of this address is 16 (1*4096/256):

```
10    A=DEC("D600"):B=A+1
20    HI=16:LO=0
30    POKE A,12:POKE B,HI
40    POKE A,13:POKE B,LO
50    POKE 2606,HI
```

The screen will be filled with garbage; this is normal. Clear the screen with PRINT CHR$(147). Now you can use this screen as you normally would. When you want to return to your old screen, change line 20 to this:

```
20    HI=0:LO=0
```

Now we're back where we started (although the cursor may not be visible, you'll be able to type).

The machine language program below uses all of the free video memory to give you three screens. It uses the interrupt, and starts immediately after execution:

Initialization:

```
1B00 78          SEI          :ignore interrupt
1B01 A9 1C       LDA #$1C
1B03 A0 18       LDY #$18
1B05 8D 15 03    STA $0315    :change interrupt pntr (lo)
1B08 8D 14 03    STA $0314    :change interrupt pntr (hi)
1B0B 58          CLI          :leave interrupt
1B0C A9 00       LDA #$00
1B0E 8D 00 10    STA $1000    :F1 cleared
```

```
1B11  8D 02 10   STA $1002   :F3 cleared
1B14  8D 04 10   STA $1004   :F5 cleared
1B17  60         RTS         :ready
```

New Interrupt

```
1B18  48         PHA         :save accumulator
1B19  8A         TXA
1B1A  48         PHA         :save X register
1B1B  A5 D5      LDA $D5     :read keyboard
1B1D  C9 58      CMP #$58    :no key?  Then go
1B1F  F0 3A      BEQ $1C5F   :to normal IRQ routine
1B21  A2 OC      LDX #$0C    :VDC register 12
1B23  C9 04      CMP #$04    :F1?
1B25  F0 0D      BEQ $1C38   :yes -- then goto $1C38
1B27  C9 05      CMP #$05    :F3?
1B29  F0 0E      BEQ $1C3D   :yes -- then goto $1C3D
1B2B  C9 06      CMP #$06    :F5? No -- then
1B2D  D0 2C      BNE $1C5F   :goto normal IRQ routine
1B2F  A9 00      LDA #$00    :screen at $0000
1B31  4C 3E 1B   JMP $1B3E   :set register
1B34  A9 10      LDA #$10    :screen at $1000
1B36  4C 3E 1B   JMP $11B3E  :set register
1B39  A9 18      LDA #$18    :screen at $1800
1B3B  4C 3E 1B   JMP $1B3E   :set register
1B3E  8E 00 D6   STX $D600   :desired register in REG 0
1B41  2C 00 D6   BIT $D600   :bit 7 set?
1B44  10 FB      BPL $1C45   :wait.  Write value
1B46  8D 01 D6   STA $D601   :in video RAM into REG 1
1B49  8D 2E 0A   STA $D601   :set pointer in zeropage
1B4C  A2 00      LDX #$0D    :VDC register 13
1B4E  A9 00      LDA #$00    :low byte =0
1B50  8E 00 D6   STX $D600   :set register
1B53  2C 00 D6   BIT $D600   :bit 7 set?
1B56  10 FB      BPL $1C57   :wait.  Write byte
1B58  8D 01 D6   STA $D601   :in video RAM into REG 1
1B5B  68         PLA         :return X register
1B5C  AA         TAX
1B5D  68         PLA         :return accumulator
1B5E  4C 65 FA   JMP $FA65   :back to IRQ routine
```

FOR BASIC programmers here is the BASIC loader.

```
10 FOR X = 6912 TO 7008
20 READ A: CS = CS + A:   POKE X,A
30 NEXT X
40 IF CS < > 9318 THEN  PRINT  CHR$ (7);:   LIST
45 SYS 6912
50 DATA 120,169,27,160,24,141,21,3,140,20,3,88
60 DATA 169,0,141,0,16,141,2,16,141,4,16,96
70 DATA 72,138,72,165,213,201,88,240,58,162,12,201
80 DATA 4,240,13,201,5,240,14,201,6,208,44,169
90 DATA 0,76,62,27,169,16,76,62,27,169,24,76
100 DATA 62,27,142,0,214,44,0,214,16,251,141,1
110 DATA 214,141,46,10,162,13,169,0,142,0,214,44
120 DATA 0,214,16,251,141,1,214,104,170,104,76,101
130 DATA 250
```

RUNning the initialization program causes our IRQ vector (Interrupt Request vector) in the second half of the routine to be added to the normal IRQ routine (the IRQ is what the computer executes every 1/60 second). This routine then gives you three separate 80 column screens to work with. You can shift screens in program mode (by pressing <F1>, <F3> or <F5>; be sure to clear each new screen before use), or in direct mode (POKE 213,4; POKE 213,5; or POKE 213,6, respectively).

1.18 MANIPULATING THE VDC 8563

Here's another feature of the new 80-column display controller. To show you that we're not praising this chip too much, there is a demonstration program below which will show you just how versatile the VDC 8563 is. At this point, you may want to review the VDC register listing in Chapter 1.7.

When we manipulate the display controller, the entire normal screen representation is put on the stack. In your experiments, you should remember a complete recovery of the VDC controller is often possible only by switching the computer off. By the same token, you won't cause any internal damage from playing with the registers.

Moving the Screen Windows

Those of you who owned VIC-20s in "the old days" remember that the entire screen could be moved around. This effect is accomplished on the 80-column C-128 using the VDC registers 2 and 7:

    02   Shifts screen window horizontally & character-wise

    07   Shifts screen window vertically & line-wise

Let's try it out:

```
10 REM MOVING THE SCREEN WINDOW
20 A=DEC("D600"):B=A+1
30 FOR X=0 TO 255
40 POKE A,2:POKE B,X
50 POKE A,7:POKE B,X
60 NEXT X
70 END
```

This listing will make the screen wander diagonally. You can return it to normal by pressing <RUN-STOP/RESTORE>.

Simulating an explosion may be more to your tastes. The quality of a game often depends on its realism; try this program out. We leave the sound effects to your discretion.

```
10   REM   EXPLOSIONS SIMULATION
15   A =  DEC ("D600"): B = A + 1
20   FOR X = 0 TO 50
30   Y =  INT ( RND (1) * 2) + 101
40   Z =  INT ( RND (1) * 2) + 31
50   POKE A,2:  POKE B,Y
60   POKE A,7:  POKE B,Z
70   NEXT X
80   POKE A,2:  POKE B,102
90   POKE A,7:  POKE B,32
```

1.19 MANIPULATING SCREEN FORMAT

You're presently in 80-column mode which, as the name implies, has 80 characters per line, and 25 lines per screen page. Let's say that we want to change this format for now. This is a relatively easy task, using VDC registers 1 and 6:

01   Characters per line   (default 80)

06   Lines per screen page (default 80)

NOTE: You can't get any more than 80 columns. Our goal, here, is to increase the number of lines on the screen using this formula:

(new number of columns) * (new number of lines) = 2000

If the total is greater or less than 2000, we may run into trouble. Try this, using 30 lines * 62 characters:

```
10      REM NEW SCREEN FORMAT 62 * 30
20      A=DEC("D600"):B=A+1
30      POKE A,1:POKE B,62
40      POKE A,6:POKE B,30
50      END
```

All this program does is change the screen format to 30 X 62. You can design any format in principle with this program. Perhaps you can make use of this in games simulating a mineshaft, or deep well, or having a sprite move offscreen.

1.20 FOR MONOCHROME MONITOR OWNERS

If you're the lucky owner of a "green screen" (or amber, or whatever), you obviously can't take advantage of the C-128's colors. At best, you get two shades of monitor color. What do you need that 2K of attribute RAM for? It's there for screen development, but in the case of monochrome output, it's just collecting dust, so to speak. If we want to use that RAM, we consult VDC register 25:

    25   Smooth Scroll horizontal

Bit 6 of this register declares whether attribute RAM is on or not:

```
10      REM DEACTIVATING ATTRIBUTE RAM
20      A=DEC("D600"):B=A+1
30      POKE A,25:POKE B,PEEK(B) AND NOT 64
```

This brief routine switches off attribute RAM ($0800 - $0FFF), and turns it over to you to use for screen memory. Naturally, this routine can also be used by RGB monitor owners who wish to do without color.

The Curtain Falls . . . .

Normally, the screen window sits within a prescribed border. These edges can be adjusted by VDC registers 34 and 35:

      34   Start of screen representation

      35   End of screen representation

Rather than go into lengthly explanations, here's a demo program:

```
10    A =  DEC ("D600"): B = A + 1
20    INPUT X,Y
30    POKE A,34:  POKE B,X
40    POKE A,35:  POKE B,X - Y
60    GOTO 20
```

The left and right borders can also be moved without disturbing screen contents. Try this:

```
10    A =  DEC ("D600"): B = A + 1
20    FOR X = 0 TO 40
30    POKE A,34:  POKE B,46 - X
40    POKE A,35:  POKE B,46 + X
50    FOR T = 1 TO 10:  NEXT T
60    NEXT X
```

1.21 THE 8x16 CHARACTER MATRIX

You played around with custom characters a few pages ago; you'll recall
that each character is built into an 8 X 8 matrix:

```
76543210
. . . . . . . .0
. . . . . . . .1
. . . . . . . .2
. . . . . . . .3
. . . . . . . .4
. . . . . . . .5
. . . . . . . .6
. . . . . . . .7
```

Now that you've had some experience in character design, you may not
want to be limited to the 8 X 8 matrix; it's too small to make a spaceship
character, and much too large for a small character. In the paragraphs to
follow, we'll show you how to change the size of the character matrix itself.

Let's peek into the registers that control matrix size (registers 22 and 23):

    22   Matrix display (horizontal)
    23   Matrix display (vertical)

Relative Changing of the Matrix

Each register lists how many pixels are in a character matrix; default of both registers is eight, governed by the first four bits of register 22 and the first five bits of register 23.

```
10    A =  DEC ("D600"): B = A + 1
20    FOR X = 0 TO 8
30    POKE A,22:  POKE B, PEEK (B) AND  NOT 7 OR X
40    FOR T = 1 TO 100:  NEXT T
50    NEXT X
60    FOR X = 0 TO 8
70    POKE A,23:  POKE B,X
71    FOR T = 1 TO 100:  NEXT T
80    NEXT X
90    END
```

Here's a neat little arrangement for game use:

```
10    A =  DEC ("D600"): B = A + 1
20    FOR X = 0 TO 8
30    POKE A,22:  POKE B, PEEK (B) AND  NOT 7 OR X
40    POKE A,23:  POKE B,X
50    FOR T = 1 TO 200:  NEXT T
60    NEXT X
70    END
```

This is only a relative size change, and leaves us with an 8 X 8 matrix, most of which simply goes unused.

1.22 TOTAL 16X8 MATRIX MANIPULATION

Let's try developing a 16X8 matrix. In other words, we'll create an 8-column matrix of 16 lines. We'll find the needed numbers at registers 4 and 9 of the VDC:

04   Vertical synchronization

09   Vertical matrix register

Register 9 declares the number of lines in a character. To raise the matrix to 16 points, we'll have to double the amount in register 9, and change the synchronization in 04:

```
10  REM 16 * 8 MATRIX
20  A=DEC("D600"):B=A+1
30  POKE 228,16
40  READ X
50  IF X=-1 THEN END
60  READ Y
70  POKEA,X:POKEB,Y
80  GOTO 20
90  :
100 DATA 9,15
110 DATA 6,17
120 DATA 23,15
130 DATA 4,19
140 DATA 7,19
150 DATA -1
```

After starting the program, the screen looks funny; there's a big space between the screen lines, but the characters are still clear. That space is due to the enlarged matrix; the space is the additional 8 pixels (see Chapter 1.12).

Type `PRINT CHR$(27)+"R"` in direct mode; this reverses the screen contents, and lets you see the scope of the character expansion. This project gives you 17 lines of 80 characters, with a 16 X 8 matrix. Let's figure out the total resolution:

```
PRINT 17*80*(16*8)
```

This gives you 174,080 pixels!! Since the video RAM is limited to 16K, these points can't be easily set (e.g. bit-mapping).

Here is the program's explanation:

10	A=VDC,B=REG 01
20	Bottom window border is set to keep cursor from scrolling offscreen.
30	VDC loaded with new value.
60	Read DATA
70	Switch character size from 8 to 16 pixels.
80	Limit to 17 lines per screen.
90	16 X 8 pixels per character.
100	20 lines (+ border) instead of 40.
110	Bring up screen contents in proper format.

1.23 DOUBLE-HEIGHT CHARACTERS

So, what can we do with that 16 X 8 matrix? We can create double-height characters, and this next program lets you do just that.

```
10     REM   POKE-ROUT
20     FOR X = 6144 TO 6182
30     READ A: CS = CS + A:   POKE X,A
40     NEXT X
50     IF CS < > 3411 THEN   PRINT "DATA-ERROR":   END
60     DATA 72,138,72,152,72,169,2,141,40,10,162,18
70     DATA 104,32,27,24,232,104,32,27,24,162,31,104
80     DATA 76,27,24,142,0,214,44,0,214,16,251
85     DATA 141,1,214,96
90     REM   COPY
100    FOR W = 0 TO 255:   REM   256 CHARS
110    FOR K = 0 TO 7:   REM   8 LINES EACH
120    AD = 53248 + W * 8 + K
130    BANK 14: K(K) =   PEEK (AD): BANK 15
140    NEXT K
150    FOR K = 0 TO 15:   REM   15 LINE SET
160    AD = 8192 + W * 16 + K
170    HI =   INT (AD / 256): LO = AD - (256 * HI)
180    SYS   DEC ("1800"),K( INT (K / 2)),LO,HI
190    NEXT K
200    NEXT W
```

This routine is *slow...* in BASIC. For impatient readers, we'll give you a machine code listing:

```
0B00 A2 03     LDX #$03      :Read loop
0B02 BD 41 0B  LDA 0B41,X    :Load starting address
0B05 95 FA     STA $FA,X     :into free zero page
0B07 DEX                     :Everything read in?
0B08 10 F8     BPL $0B02     :No -- continue
0B0A A2 01     LDX #$01      :Set bank
0B0C 8E 00 FF  STX $FF00     :configuration
0B0F A0 00     LDY #$00      :to 0+vector
```

```
0B11 B1 FA       LDA ($FA),Y       :Read in start address
0B13 48          PHA               :Get it
0B14 A2 00       LDX #$00          :Set bank
0B16 8E 00 FF    STX $FF00         :configuration
0B19 A6 FC       LDX $FC           :Low video RAM address
0B1B A4 FD       LDY $FD           :High video RAM address
0B1D 20 46 0B    JSR $0B46         :POKE subroutine
0B20 E6 FC       INC $FC           :Low=Low+1
0B22 D0 02       BNE $0B26         :Low greater than 0
0B24 E6 FD       INC $FD           :Low=0:High=High+1
0B26 68          PLA               :Get High ROM
0B27 A6 FC       LDX $FC           :Low video RAM address
0B29 A4 FD       LDY $FD           :High video RAM address
0B2B 20 46 0B    JSR $0B46         :POKE subroutine
0B2E E6 FC       INC $FC           :Low=Low+1
0B30 D0 02       BNE $0B34         :Low greater than 0
0B32 E6 FD       INC $FD           :Low=0:High=High+1
0B34 E6 FA       INC $FA           :Low ROM=Low ROM+1
0B36 D0 02       BNE $0B3A         :Still >0?  NO--
0B38 E6 FB       INC $FB           :High ROM=High ROM+1
0B3A A4 FB       LDY $FB           :Load
0B3C C0 E0       CPY #$E0          :Reached end of ROM
0B3E 90 CA       BCC $0B0A         :yet?  NO--go on
0B40 60          RTS               :Return to BASIC
0B41 00 D0 00 20 00                :Pntr starting address
0B46 48          PHA               :Get character
0B47 8A          TXA
0B48 48          PHA               :Get low byte
0B49 98          TYA
0B4A 48          PHA               :Get high byte
0B4B A9 02       LDA #$02
0B4D 8D 28 0A    STA $0A28         :Set cursor flag
0B50 A2 12       LDX #$12          :VDC REG 18
0B52 68          PLA               :Set low byte of
0B53 20 61 0B    JSR $0B61         :register
0B56 E8          INX               :VDC REG 19
0B57 68          PLA               :Set high byte
0B58 20 61 0B    JSR $0B61         :of register
0B5B A2 1F       LDX #$1F          :VDC REG 31
0B5D 68          PLA               :Character
0B5E 4C 61 0B    JMP $0B61         :Register set, ready
0B61 8E 00 D6    STX $D600         :Desired register given
0B64 2C 00 D6    BIT $D600         :Bit 7 set?
```

```
0B67 10 FB     BPL $0B64      :NO--then wait
0B69 8D 01 D6  STA $D601      :for given value
0B6C 60        RTS            :Return
```

There is, of course, a matching BASIC loader:

```
5000    FOR X = 2816 TO 2924
5010    READ A: CS = CS + A:   POKE X,A
5020    NEXT X
5030    IF CS <> 13689 THEN PRINT CHR$ (7);: LIST
5040    DATA 162,3,189,65,11,149,250,202,16,248,162,1
5050    DATA 142,0,255,160,0,177,250,72,162,0,142,0
5060    DATA 255,166,252,164,253,32,70,11,230,252,208,2
5070    DATA 230,253,104,166,252,164,253,32,70,11,230,252
5080    DATA 208,2,230,253,230,250,208,2,230,251,164,251
5090    DATA 192,224,144,202,96,0,208,0,32,0,72,138
5100    DATA 72,152,72,169,2,141,40,10,162,18,104,32
5110    DATA 97,11,232,104,32,97,11,162,31,104,76,97
5120    DATA 11,142,0,214,44,0,214,16,251,141,1,214
5130    DATA 96
```

Defining the 16 X 8 Matrix

Let's continue by defining some 16 X 8 characters. This procedure has already been covered in the chapter on "Designing your own Characters". Make the following corrections in the 80 column character editor program:

```
2 MA=15
5055 FOR Y=0 TO 15
```

1.24 MOVING THE VIDEO RAM

Video RAM is divided into four sections:

> $0000   2K Screen memory
> $0800   2K Attribute RAM
> $1000   Free
> $2000   8K Character generator

You'll find the purpose of the free 4K ($1000) in Chapter1.17; for the moment, we're talking about the other three areas. It's possible to move attribute RAM and screen RAM in 256-byte steps, while the character generator can only be moved 8K at a time. Here are the VDC's registers for controlling this:

>   12   HIgh byte of screen memory
>   13   LOw byte of screen memory
>   20   HIgh byte - attribute RAM
>   21   LOw byte - attribute RAM
>   28   HIgh byte - character generator (bits 5-7)

Moving Attribute RAM

The program below moves attribute RAM into any area of video RAM. Please note that you are limited to 256-byte steps.

```
10      REM ATTRIBUTE RAM SHIFTER
20      INPUT "NEW STARTING ADDRESS";AD$
25      AD=DEC(AD$)
30      IF AD/256=INT(AD/256)THEN 40:ELSE PRINT
        "256K STEPS!":GOTO 20
40      HI=INT(AD/256):LO=AD-(256*HI)
50      A=DEC("D600"):B=A+1
60      POKE A,20:POKE B,HI
70      POKE A,21:POKE B,LO
80      POKE 2607,HI
```

The value at line 80 is a special number; it's not enough to simply change the VDC registers or they will remain unchanged. At the same time, a specified address in zero page will be loaded with the high-byte of the new starting address:

   2606 :HIgh byte of screen RAM

   2607 :HIgh byte of attribute RAM

Try the address "1000"; attribute RAM is moved to the free area. Type a few different characters on the screen and see what you get. Now, run the attribute RAM shifter routine again, and specify "800" as a starting address. The characters take on normal color again.

You can actually use this technique in page-flipping routines (i.e., set up a different color memory on each screen page, and switch back and forth). We suggest the addresses between "1000" and "1800" as the most suitable.

Just to show you what happens when you enter an illegal address, run the attribute RAM shifter program again, and enter "0000", which will put attribute RAM in the same range as screen RAM. The result: every character has its own color and shape!

Or enter "2000", which puts us in the character generator; certain characters lose their normal appearance.

Moving Screen RAM

This function is analogous to moving attribute RAM. You'll find the important addresses in the preceding sections.

We believe that shifting screen RAM is a useful extra, since it allows you to perform the page-flipping trick (see Chapter 1.17).

1.25 COLOR FOR THE 80-COLUMN SCREEN

Color? You bet! 80-column mode gives you a choice of 16 character colors, by using <CTRL 1-8> and <C= 1-8>. For now, though, we'll concern ourselves with changing the border and background colors. There too we have 16 colors to choose from, but we'll have to POKE the colors in. In 40-column mode addresses 53280 and 53281 are used; 80-column mode utilizes register 26 of the VDC for background. Here's what you do to change register 26:

```
POKE DEC("D600"),26:POKE DEC("D601"),X     [X=COLOR]
```

You could use color control characters within a PRINT statement, but it's not the best method. POKEing the color into address 241 is a better method:

```
POKE 241,X [X=COLOR NUMBER FROM 0 TO 15]
```

Look for a moment at the last four bits of a byte in attribute RAM:

    BIT 4: blinking
    BIT 5: underscored
    BIT 6: reverse video
    BIT 7: 2nd character set

It was once quite difficult to get these functions; the only way you could implement some of these functions was by programming them yourself.

Two methods of accessing the second character set are to press <C=> and <SHIFT> simultaneously, or to use a PRINT character string. These other functions still aren't very simple to get at, but programming them has gotten a lot easier.

```
POKE 241,PEEK(241) OR 2^4:PRINT"THIS LINE BLINKS!"
```

```
POKE 241,PEEK(241) OR 2^5:PRINT "UNDERSCORED!"
```

Here's a sample program:

```
10 PRINT "THIS MATTER IS ";
20 POKE 241,PEEK(241)OR 2^5
30 PRINT"IMPORTANT";
40 POKE 241,PEEK(241) AND NOT 2^5
50 PRINT"!"
60 END
```

The word IMPORTANT will blink if you replace 2^5 with 2^4. Using "2^5+2^4" instead of 2^5 alone will simultaneously underline *and* blink the word.   Naturally, 2^6 will bring up reverse video, and 2^7 will call the second character set.

1.26 CUSTOM CHARACTER GENERATOR

Earlier in this section, we explained the design of the character generator used by the 80-column controller. You'll also remember our mentioning that each character has a 16 X 8 matrix. We have already used these 16 bytes in 16 X 8 definition. We'd like to take that a step further.

Let's assume that you start with a normal 8 X 8 matrix. Only 8 bytes are used in character definition, with the remaining 8 bytes hiding somewhere in the background. The machine language routine below (we call it "Swapper") trades off one set of 8 bytes for the other set. This means that you can design another character set, and switch off between "standard" and your own custom characters.

```
0B00 A9 00     LDA #$00     :Store first low byte
0B02 85 4C     STA $4C      :pointer
0B04 A9 20     LDA #$20     :Store first high byte
0B06 85 4D     STA $4D      :pointer
0B08 A9 08     LDA #$08     :Store second low byte
0B0A 85 43     STA #$4E     :pointer
0B0C A9 20     LDA #$20     :Store second high byte
0B0E 85 4F     STA $4F      :pointer
0B10 A0 07     LDY #$07     :8 bytes
0B12 98        TYA
0B13 48        PHA          :on stack
0B14 A5 4C     LDA $4C      :Low byte of first pointer
```

```
0B16 A6 4D       LDX $4D      :Hi-byte of first pointer
0B18 20 8C 0B    JSR $0B8C    :PEEK subroutine
0B1B 48          PHA          :Put char. on stack
0B1C A5 4E       LDA $4E      :Lo-byte of second pointer
0B1E A6 4F       LDX $4F      :Hi-byte of second pointer
0B20 20 8C 0B    JSR $0B8C    :PEEK subroutine
0B23 A6 4C       LDX $4C      :Low byte of first pointer
0B25 A4 4D       LDY $4D      :Hi-byte of first pointer
0B27 20 65 0B    JSR $0B65    :POKE subroutine
0B2A 68          PLA          :Read character
0B2B A6 4E       LDX $4E      :Lo-byte of second pointer
0B2D A4 4F       LDY $4F      :Hi-byte of second pointer
0B2F 20 65 0B    JSR $0B65    :POKE subroutine
0B32 E6 4C       INC $4C      :Low byte 1=Low byte 1+1
0B34 D0 02       BNE $0B3E    :Still >0?
0B36 E6 4D       INC $4D      :NO--High 1=High 1+1
0B38 E6 4E       INC $4E      :Low byte 2=Low byte 2+1
0B3A D0 02       BNE $0B3E    :Still >0?
0B3C E6 4F       INC $4F      :NO--High 2=High 2+1
0B3E 68          PLA          :Back to read-in value
0B3F A8          TAY
0B40 88          DEY
0B41 10 CF       BPL $0B12    :Copy more
0B43 A5 4F       LDA $4F      :Hi-byte of second pointer
0B45 C9 40       CMP #$40     :reached $4000 yet?
0B47 B0 1B       BCS $0B64    :YES--ready
0B49 A9 08       LDA #$08     :Low=Low+ 8 char. bytes
0B4B 65 4C       ADC $4C      :added
0B4D 85 4C       STA $4C      :Store some more
0B4F A9 00       LDA #$00     :add 0
0B51 65 4D       ADC $4D      :add carry
0B53 85 4D       STA $4D      :Store some more
0B55 A9 08       LDA #$08     :Low2=Low2+8 char. bytes
0B57 65 4E       ADC $4E      :added
0B59 85 4E       STA $4E      :Store some more
0B5B A9 00       LDA #$00     :add 0
0B5D 65 4F       ADC $4F      :add carry
0B5F 85 4F       STA $4F      :Store some more
0B61 4C 10 0B    JMP $0B10    :Loop
0B64 60          RTS          :Go back to BASIC
0B65 48          PHA          :Hold char.
0B66 8A          TXA
0B67 48          PHA          :Get low byte
```

```
0B68 98           TYA
0B69 48           PHA             :Get high byte
0B6A A9 02        LDA #$02
0B6C 8D 28 0A     STA $0A28       :Set cursor flag
0B6F A2 12        LDX #$12        :VDC REG 18
0B71 68           PLA             :Put back high byte
0B72 20 80 0B     JSR $0B80       :Set register
0B75 E8           INX             :VDC REG 19
0B76 68           PLA             :Get low-byte
0B77 20 80 0B     JSR $0B80       :Set register
0B7A A2 1F        LDX #$1F        :VDC REG 31
0B7C 68           PLA             :Get byte
0B7D 4C 80 0B     JMP $0B80       :Ready; set register
0B80 8E 00 D6     STX $D600       :REG set
0B83 2C 00 D6     BIT $D600       :Wait
0B86 10 FB        BPL $0B83       :Waited long enough?
0B88 8D 01 D6     STA $D601       :Value given
0B8B 60           RTS             :Ready
0B8C 48           PHA             :Get low byte
0B8D 8A           TXA
0B8E 48           PHA             :Get high byte
0B8F A2 12        LDX #$12        :REG 18 VDC
0B91 68           PLA             :High byte in accumulator
0B92 20 80 0B     JSR $0B80       :Set register
0B95 E8           INX             :REG 19 VDC
0B96 68           PLA             :Low byte in accumulator
0B97 20 80 0B     JSR $0B80       :Set register
0B9A A2 1F        LDX #$1F        :REG 31 VDC
0B9C 8E 00 D6     STX $D600       :Set register
0B9F 2C 00 D6     BIT $D600       :Wait
0BA2 10 FB        BPL 0B9F        :Long enough?
0BA4 AD 01 D6     LDA $D601       :Read value from video RAM
0BA7 85 FE        STA $FE         :Put on
0BA9 60           RTS             :Ready
```

Here's the matching BASIC loader.

```
5000    FOR X = 2816 TO 2985
5010    READ A: CS = CS + A:    POKE X,A
5020    NEXT X
5030    IF CS <> 17057 THEN PRINT CHR$ (7);:   LIST
5040    DATA 169,0,133,76,169,32,133,77,169,8,133,78
5050    DATA 169,32,133,79,160,7,152,72,165,76,166,77
5060    DATA 32,140,11,72,165,78,166,79,32,140,11,166
5070    DATA 76,164,77,32,101,11,104,166,78,164,79,32
5080    DATA 101,11,230,76,208,2,230,77,230,78,208,2
5090    DATA 230,79,104,168,136,16,207,165,79,201,64,176
5100    DATA 27,169,8,101,76,133,76,169,0,101,77,133
5110    DATA 77,169,8,101,78,133,78,169,0,101,79,133
5120    DATA 79,76,16,11,96,72,138,72,152,72,169,2
5130    DATA 141,40,10,162,18,104,32,128,11,232,104,32
5140    DATA 128,11,162,31,104,76,128,11,142,0,214,44
5150    DATA 0,214,16,251,141,1,214,96,72,138,72,162
5160    DATA 18,104,32,128,11,232,104,32,128,11,162,31
5170    DATA 142,0,214,44,0,214,16,251,173,1,214,133
5180    DATA 254,96
```

RUNning the routine by typing SYS DEC("0B00") turns the screen black, after which the cursor reappears.

The character generator will be switched in the normal manner. The second set of eight bytes per character would normally read null. So, switching the character gives you spaces to define. You can call back the original character set by calling the routine again. Now load the character editor in Chapter 1.16; you can produce new characters to your heart's content. One small change will have to be made in the BASIC program, though, at line 5065:

```
5065 AD=8192+16*A+Y+8
```

Now start the loader. Swap your character generators with the routine, and go to it.   You can also have two self-defined character sets, rather than one "standard" and one "custom" (for games, etc.).

1.27 SYSTEM ROUTINES

Maybe you've been looking for special routines to use with 80-column mode, like instant access to video RAM, or controller initialization. Well, the built-in ROM routines for the 40-column screen aren't limited to that mode (the operating system works on both screens). It's possible, then, to use the built-in ROM routines in 80-column mode through programming.

Now, on to the routines themselves. Each routine has two addresses; the first is the jump table for the editor, while the second is the starting address of the routine proper. Which address you use is up to you.

Screen Initialization

The following routine initializes the screen, somewhat akin to using <RUN-STOP/RESTORE>:

```
SYS 49152/SYS 49275
```

Color Output of a Character

This was mentioned in Chapter 1.9. in connection with the 80-column screen. The routine simply prints a character of a specified color on the screen, with the position depending on the contents of locations 224 and 225:

```
SYS 49155,CHAR,COLOR
SYS 52276,CHAR,COLOR
```

CHAR: (0-255) Character in screen code (A=1,B=2,etc.)
COLOR:(0-15) Color the character should be (0=black,1=white, etc.)
              80-column mode also allows values from 0 to 255. The
              additional 4 bits have these meanings:

BIT 4:	Blinking
BIT 5:	Underscore
BIT 6:	Reverse video
BIT 7:	2nd character set

ASCII Output

The preceding subsection mentioned the "screen code". This code is Commodore-specific, and *not* standard—but you can get ASCII output like this:

```
SYS 49164, ASCII code
SYS 50989, ASCII code
PRINT CHR$(ASCII code)
```

Conversely, you can find out the ASCII code by typing:

```
PRINT ASC("K")
```

which would give us the ASCII code number for K.

PRINT AT Simulation

Basically, this routine lets you format things on screen (called PRINT AT in some BASIC versions). Here is a command which works in conjunction with the machine language call CHAR:

```
SYS 49176,A,column, row:PRINT...
SYS 52330,A,column, row:PRINT...
```

You could conceivably use this to display a command line onscreen (with warnings and system status addressed to the user). You see this a lot on professional software; now you can have it in a user-friendly atmosphere.

If you want to see just where the PRINT AT command has written an item, check these locations:

```
10 REM PRINT AT WITH RETURN
20 SP=PEEK(236):REM CURRENT COLUMN STORED
30 ZE=PEEK(235):REM CURRENT ROW STORED
40 :
50 SYS 49176,0,5,10:PRINT"COMMAND LINE"
60 :
70 SYS 49176,0,SP,ZE:REM BACK AGAIN
80 PRINT"BACK THERE"
90 END
```

All this routine needs to do is get the current cursor position from the operating system.

Definition of Character Sets

This routine is for the 80-column mode only. If, by some chance, you don't like your custom character set, or it doesn't work very well, this routine copies the original character set into the VDC's video RAM.

```
SYS 49191 / SYS 52748
```

40/80-Column Toggling

We've mentioned this little trick before:

```
SYS 49194 / SYS 52526
```

For more information on these routines, please see Chapter 11.2: The Kernal.

1.28 HIGH-RESOLUTION GRAPHICS

The C-128 has a new BASIC (BASIC 7.0), with a host of graphic commands to make hi-res programming easier. Trouble is, the hi-res commands only operate in 40-column mode. We don't understand why you can't use them in 80-column mode; the doubled resolution (640*200 pixels) would come in handy.

The following pages will show you how to do 80-column hi-res graphics, and how to use this in your programs. If you're without an RGB monitor, you'll have to amuse yourself with standard graphic commands.

Bit-Map Mode

Those of you former C-64 and VIC-20 owners probably remember "bit-map mode" in high-resolution programming: Essentially, it switches the screen from normal to high-resolution mode. Video RAM is no longer divided into screen memory, attribute RAM and the character generator. The computer works bit-for-bit with video RAM. In other words, for every set (on) bit, a point is written to the screen.

Our 80-column screen would give us a resolution along the lines of:

```
16000 BYTES * 8 BITS = 128,000 SCREEN POINTS
```

--which you can have either set or unset.

Switching on the bit-map mode is accomplished by registers 20 and 25:

        20   Attribute RAM starting address (HIGH)

        25   Bit 7: Hi-Res On/Off

Let's turn the bit-map on with this little program:

```
10 A=DEC("D600"):B=A+1
20 POKE A,20:POKE B,0
30 POKE A,25:POKE B,128
```

Immediately, the screen is a jumble of points and lines. There is method to this madness, though: every bit in the 16K of video RAM has been switched ON. Using the modified Poke routine from Chapter 1.10, try this:


```
SYS DEC("1800"),128,0,0
```

That turns one point on at the upper left-hand corner of the screen. Now that you have the principle, here's a program that draws a sine wave on the screen. The PLOT routine works faster than some machine code routines; it manages this through a) the modified POKE (see "POKE Simulation"), b) the modified PEEK, and c) ERASE (clearing the graphic screen).

Type this program in first and start it; it's the graphics initialization routine.

```
10    FOR X = 6144 TO 6182
20    READ A : CS = CS + A : POKE X, A
30    NEXT X
40    IF CS <> 3411 THEN PRINT "DATA ERROR IN 40"
50    DATA 72, 138,72,152,72,169,2,141,40,10,162,18
60    DATA 104,32,27,24,232,104,32,27,24,162,31,104
70    DATA 76,27,24,142,0,214,44,0,214,16,251,141
80    DATA 1,214,96
```

```
85    CS = 0
90    FOR X = 6656 TO 6697
100   READ A: CS = CS + A:  POKE X,A
110   NEXT X
120   IF CS <> 4356 THEN  PRINT "DATA ERROR IN 120"
130   DATA 72,138,72,162,18,104,32,30,26,232,104,32
140   DATA 30,26,162,31,142,0,214,44,0,214,16,251
150   DATA 173,1,214,133,254,96,142,0,214,44,0,214
160   DATA 16,251,141,1,214,96
165   CS = 0
170   FOR X = 6400 TO 6453
180   READ A: CS = CS + A:  POKE X,A
190   NEXT X
200   IF CS <> 6426 THEN  PRINT "DATA ERROR IN 200"
210   DATA 162,64,169,0,160,0,133,254,72,138,72,162
220   DATA 18,165,254,32,42,25,232,152,32,42,25,162
230   DATA 31,169,0,32,42,25,104,170,104,200,208
240   DATA 228,230,254,202,208,223,96,142,0,214,44
250   DATA  0,214,16,251,141,1,214,96
```

And now for the sine wave:

```
10    REM   80 COL SINE WAVE PLOT PROGRAM
20    A =   DEC ("D600"): B = A + 1
30    REM   PLOT:SYS DEC("1800"),BYTE,LO,HI
40    REM   ERASE:SYS DEC("1900")
50    REM   PEEK:SYS DEC("1A00"),LO,HI:
            PRINT PEEK(254);
60    :
70    POKE A,25:  POKE B,128:  POKE A,20:  POKE B,0
80    SYS   DEC ("1900")
110   FOR X = 0 TO 639
120   Y =   INT ( SIN (X / 10) * 100) + 100
130   GOSUB 170
140   NEXT X
150   END
170   REM   PLOT
180   AN = 80 * Y
190   Z1 =   INT (X / 8)
200   AD = AN + Z1: HI =INT (AD/256):LO =AD-256 * HI
210   SYS   DEC ("1A00"),LO,HI
220   PE =   PEEK (254) OR 2 ^ (7 - (X - Z1 * 8))
```

```
230 SYS  DEC ("1800"),PE,LO,HI
240 RETURN
```

The modified POKE has been described previously. Here is the ERASE
routine:

```
1900 A2 40       LDX #$40     :Clear 64 pages
1902 A9 00       LDA #$00     :from $0000
1904 A0 00       LDY #$00
1906 85 FE       STA $FE      :Store high byte
1908 48          PHA          :and retrieve
1909 8A          TXA
190A 48          PHA          :Retrieve pages
190B A2 12       LDX #$12     :VDC REG 18
190D A5 FE       LDA $FE      :Load high-byte
190F 20 2A 19    JSR $192A    :Set register
1912 E8          INX          :VDC REG 19
1913 98          TYA          :Low byte into accumulator
1914 20 2A 19    JSR $192A    :Set register
1917 A2 1F       LDX #$1F     :VDC REG 31
1919 A9 00       LDA #$00     :Write 0 into video RAM
191B 20 2A 19    JSR $192A    :Set register
191E 68          PLA          :Get high byte
191F AA          TAX          :in X-register
1920 68          PLA          :Get pages
1921 C8          INY
1922 D0 E4       BNE $1908    :Loop
1924 E6 FE       INC $FE      :High=High+1
1926 CA          DEX          :Page=Page-1
1927 D0 DF       BNE $1908    :Still >0?  Keep going.
1929 60          RTS          :Return to BASIC
192A 8E 00 D6    STX $D600    :Set register
192D 2C 00 D6    BIT $D600    :Wait
1930 10 FB       BPL $192D    :Waited long enough?
1932 80 01 D6    STA $D601    :Value given
1935 60          RTS          :Return
```

These graphic commands aren't exactly the fastest. It won't be long,
though, before someone brings out an 80-column graphic extension.

1.29 CHARACTER GENERATORS—AGAIN

We close with a short program that will perform a headstand—literally. We suggest that you review the POKE routine ($1800) and PEEK routine ($1A00) in the previous chapters. The graphic initialization routine from page 65 must first be loaded and run.

Here's one for the normal 8 X 8 matrix:

```
10  FOR X = 0 TO 511
20  FOR X2 = 0 TO 3
30  A1 =8199+8*X-X2: H1= INT(A1/256): L1= A1-256*H1
40  SYS  DEC ("1A00"),L1,H1
50  W1 =  PEEK ( DEC ("FE"))
60  A2 =8192+8*X+X2: H2 =INT(A2/256): L2 =A2-256*H2
70  SYS  DEC ("1A00"),L2,H2
80  W2 =  PEEK ( DEC ("FE"))
90  SYS  DEC ("1800"),W2,L1,H1
100 SYS  DEC ("1800"),W1,L2,H2
110 NEXT X2
120 NEXT X
```

And here's one for the 16 X 8 matrix (Note: you must have previously defined a 16 X 8 matrix to see the results of this program):

```
10   FOR X = 0 TO 511
20   FOR X2 = 0 TO 7
30   A1 =8207+16*X-X2: H1=INT(A1/256):L1=A1-256*H1
40   SYS  DEC ("1A00"),L1,H1
50   W1 =  PEEK ( DEC ("FE"))
60   A2=8192+16*X+X2: H2=INT(A2/256):L2=A2-256*H2
70   SYS  DEC ("1A00"),L2,H2
80   W2 =  PEEK ( DEC ("FE"))
90   SYS  DEC ("1800"),W2,L1,H1
100  SYS  DEC ("1800"),W1,L2,H2
110  NEXT X2
120  NEXT X
```

CHAPTER 2

BASIC 7.0 GRAPHICS COMMANDS

2.1 THE CIRCLE COMMAND

CIRCLE is one of the most versatile commands in BASIC 7.0. As its name suggests, it can draw circles. But it can also draw lines, triangles, rectangles, ellipses and other geometric shapes. The command uses the following format:

```
CIRCLE clr,x,y,xr,xy,sa,ea,r,i
```

These parameters are defined as follows::

clr	Number of color memory (0-3)
x,y	Coordinates for center point
xr	Radius in x-direction
yr	Radius in y-direction
sa	Starting angle of the circle
ea	End angle of the circle
r	Angle for rotation
i	Angle for drawn circle segments

To draw a circle use the first four parameters; the rest are for finer details, as we shall soon see. The first value gives color memory; the next two indicate midpoint coordinates; and the next, the radius.

Drawing an ellipse requires the previous coordinates, plus the Y-register radius (if unequal to the X-register radius):

```
CIRCLE 0,160,100,10,30
```

If you wish to turn the ellipse at the midpoint, you'll have to change the last value. For example:

```
CIRCLE 0,160,100,10,30,0,360,45
```

These parameters give the number of degrees drawn of the ellipse/circle. The sixth and seventh values tell at which angles the circle/ellipse begins and ends. We can get a half-circle by doing this:

```
CIRCLE 0,160,100,30,30,0,180
```

How can we get squares out of this command? The last parameter performs that function, using these numbers:

0-44	Circle (higher the number, the "rounder")
45	Octagon
60	Hexagon
75	Pentagon
90	Square & Rectangle
91-119	Unequal rectangle
120	Equilateral triangle
121-179	Triangle (higher the value, the more unequal)
180-255	Lines

2.2 PIE CHARTS

BASIC 7.0's graphic commands offer a lot to the user. One of the little extensions of the CIRCLE command that we've written is a fascinating one: PIE CHARTS. You can imagine how useful this program can be for calculation programs, statistics and the like. Naturally, our routine isn't as good as something "store-bought"; we'll leave it to you to improve it....

Now on to the program. One problem that cropped up was the fact that the color memory in hi-res mode isn't the same size as the graphic memory. So, we had to color in an entire field with 8 X 8 points. We could have used multicolor mode instead, but then we would have ended up with a pie with sharp edges.

These problems only occur in every other segment. You can turn segment colors off altogether (delete 340-390) to avoid some of these difficulties.

```
10    REM  PIE CHARTS
20    GRAPHIC 0,1
30    INPUT "SEGMENT SIZE";N
35    IF N = 0 THEN   END
40    DIM A(N)
45    DIM P(N)
50    DIM T$(N)
60    FOR I = 1 TO N
70    PRINT I". SEGMENT"
80    INPUT "VALUE";A(I)
90    P = P + A(I)
100   INPUT "TEXT ";T$(I)
110   NEXT I
120   INPUT "ANY CHANGES (Y/N) ";A$
130   IF  LEFT$ (A$,1) = "Y" THEN BEGIN
140   FOR I = 1 TO N
150   PRINT I".   "T$(I),A(I)
```

```
160    NEXT I
170    INPUT "SEGMENT NUMBER ";I
180    P = P - A(I)
190    INPUT "VALUE";A(I)
200    P = P + A(I)
210    INPUT "TEXT ";T$(I)
220    GOTO 120
230    BEND
240    REM  DRAW PIE CHART
250    GRAPHIC 1,1
260    COLOR 1,1
270    CIRCLE ,160,100,80
280    G = 0
290    FOR I = 1 TO N
300    P(I) = A(I) / P * 100
310    G = G + P(I)
320    CIRCLE ,160,100,80,0,0,80,G * 3.6
330    IF I / 2 <  >  INT (I / 2) THEN 520
340    REM  DRAW SEGMENTS
350    COLOR 1,I / 2 + .5
360    CIRCLE ,160,100,80,0,0,40,G * 3.6-P(I) * 1.8
370    X =  RDOT (0)
380    Y =  RDOT (1)
390    PAINT ,X + 2,Y + 1
400    NEXT I
410    REM  TEXT PRINT
420    G = 0
430    FOR I = 1 TO N
440    G = G + P(I)
450    COLOR 1,I / 2 + .5
460    CIRCLE ,160,100,80,0,89,90,G * 3.6-P(I)  * 1.8
470    COLOR 1,1
480    X =  RDOT (0) / 8
490    Y =  RDOT (1) / 8
500    IF X < 16 THEN X = X -  LEN (T$(I))
510    CHAR ,X,Y,T$(I)+STR$(INT(10*P(I) + .5) / 10)
520    NEXT I
525    CHAR ,14,24,"'SPACE' TO CONT."
530    GET  KEY A$
540    GRAPHIC 0
550    PRINT "{RVS ON}N{RVS OFF}EW PIE CHART"
555    PRINT "{RVS ON}O{RVS OFF}LD PIE CHART"
556    PRINT "'SPACE' TO END"
```

```
560    GET  KEY A$
570    IF A$ = "N" THEN  RUN
580    IF A$ = "O" THEN 120
```

The input of different portions results with absolute values and not percentages; every portion can include a text string of your choice (as long as it's not too large a string).

2.3 BAR GRAPHS

Let's go on to another graphic aid for calculation programs: Bar graphs. Our programs are limited to 8 "blocks" per character block (it loses something on the 40- character screen). Block length is up to you; and the highest value would be 100 (as in percent). You'll note that we've taken great advantage of the vertical resolution (you'll find the calculations in line 280).

```
10      REM  BAR GRAPHS
20      GRAPHIC 0
30      SCNCLR
40      DIM A(8)
50      DIM F(8)
60      INPUT "GRAPH NAME";U$
70      U$ = "        " + U$
80      FOR I =  LEN (U$) TO 39
90      U$ = U$ + " "
100     NEXT I
110     INPUT "NUMBER OF BARS (1-8)";D
120     IF D < 1 OR D > 8 THEN 110
130     FOR I = 1 TO D
140     PRINT "BAR #"I
150     INPUT "HOW MUCH";A(I)
160     IF A(I) > MAX THEN MAX = A(I)
170     INPUT "COLOR (1-16)";F(I)
180     IF F(I) < 1 OR F(I) > 16 THEN 170
```

```
190      NEXT I
200      PRINT "USE THIS DATA?"
210      GET  KEY A$
220      IF A$ = "N" THEN  RUN
230      GRAPHIC 1
240      SCNCLR
250      COLOR 1,1
260      CHAR ,0,0,U$,1
270      FOR I = 1 TO D
280      A(I) = 190 - A(I) / MAX * 170
290      COLOR 1,F(I)
300      BOX ,I * 38 - 24,A(I),I * 38,190,0,1
310      DRAW ,I*38-24,A(I) TO I*38-18,A(I)-6 TO I*38
         + 6,A(I)-6 TO I*38 + 6,184 TO I*38,190
320      DRAW ,I * 38,A(I) TO I * 38 + 6,A(I) - 6
330      NEXT I
340      GET  KEY A$
350      GRAPHIC 0
360      SCNCLR
370      PRINT "(O) OLD GRAPH"
380      PRINT "(N) NEW GRAPH"
390      PRINT "(X) EXIT"
400      GET  KEY A$
410      IF A$ = "X" THEN  END
420      IF A$ = "O" THEN  GRAPHIC 1:  GOTO 340
430      IF A$ = "N" THEN  RUN
440      GOTO 370
```

2.4 FUNCTION PLOTTER

Who hasn't wished for smooth arcs? maximum-minimum curve representations? or the endless mysteries of a tangent? This program is a complete curve plotter. It takes your input, and plots it:

```
10    REM  FUNCTION PLOTTER
20    GRAPHIC 0,1
30    DEF  FN Y(X) =  COS (X)
40    INPUT "BEGINNING FUNCTION RANGE ";A
50    INPUT "ENDING FUNCTION RANGE   ";E
60    IF A =  > E THEN 40
70    INPUT "REGISTER  X-VALUE ";A1
80    INPUT "REGISTER  Y-VALUE ";E1
90    IF A1 =  > E1 THEN 70
100   S = (E - A) / 320
110   S2 = (E1 - A1)
120   GRAPHIC 1,1
130   FOR I = 0 TO 319
140   A = A + S
150   X = 200 - ( FN Y(A) - A1) / S2 * 199
160   IF X =  < 199 AND X =  > 0 THEN  DRAW 1,I,X
170   NEXT I
180   GET  KEY A$
190   GRAPHIC 0
```

After RUNning the program, it will prompt you for four values: the range in which the function will begin and end (be sure it's only as big as your screen); the X-register (-5 to 9); and the Y-register (0 to 9).

If you wish to explore other functions, change line 30. To get a sine wave, do this:

```
30 DEF FN Y(X)= SIN(X)
```

This will not calculate in degrees, but in radians (360 degrees are exactly 2 * PI radians). Two ground rules: X- value must be no less than 0 and no more than 3.1415; and the Y-value can only be between -1 and 1.

2.5 WINDOWS

Windows are the newest buzzword in computerese. No new computer, no new BASIC, is without this feature; and the C-128 is no exception. Unfortunately, you only get one window on the C-128; but it is possible to get multiple windows with a little finagling.

2.5.1 HOW TO DO WINDOWS

You've learned from your handbook that a window can be set up in direct mode; no problem there, but how do you find it? The borders of the window can be found by moving the cursor around. The simplest method to get out of the window space is to use <RUN-STOP/RESTORE>, which dumps the window. These methods have the disadvantage of stopping a running program. We have an answer. Isn't a window just a small screen, and a screen an enlarged window? Well, we could conceivably draw the window to fit the screen:

```
WINDOW 0,0,79,24 (80-col. screen)
WINDOW 0,0,39,24 (40-col. screen)
```

2.5.2 READING WINDOW COORDINATES

You have already heard of the command RWINDOW. You can determine the row (RWINDOW(0)), column (RWINDOW(1)) and character mode (RWINDOW(2)). If you want complete coordinates, you'll need to handle the matter a bit differently. Zero page memory has four extra bytes in which the coordinates for the current window are stored; these are addresses 228-231:

```
10 WINDOW 1,11,20,22
20 PRINT "BOTTOM BORDER:";PEEK(228)
30 PRINT "TOP    BORDER:";PEEK(229)
40 PRINT "LEFT   BORDER:";PEEK(230)
50 PRINT "RIGHT  BORDER:";PEEK(231)
```

To experiment with this program, hit <RUN-STOP/RESTORE> and change the window parameters.

2.5.3 SETTING UP ALTERNATE WINDOWS

We mentioned earlier that the screen can only have one window, as indicated by locations 228 ($E4) to 231 ($E7). Here are the default values:

```
228 ($E4)    :24
229 ($E5)    : 0
230 ($E6)    : 0
231 ($E7)    :79 (80-col. mode)
             :39 (40-col. mode)
```

Now, if you type in WINDOW 1,2,3,14 -- those values will change to the values following, regardless of screen size:

```
228  ($E4)    :14
229  ($E5)    : 2
230  ($E6)    : 1
231  ($E7)    : 3
```

You can manage machine language programming of windows, just by altering 228 to 231 decimal. POKE 228,10, for example, sets the bottom at 10.

Warning: You will run into problems if you try making windows larger than the screen.

2.5.4 VERTICAL SCROLLING

The WINDOW command allows you to produce vertical scrolling without hassles. The program looks like this:

```
10  INPUT "TEXT";A$
20  INPUT"SPEED";G
30  WINDOW 10,10,10,20
40  FOR I=1TO LEN(A$)
50  PRINT MID$(A$,I,1)
60  FOR T=1 TO G
70  NEXT T
80  NEXT I
90  GOTO 40
```

The window width is reduced to one, so the characters scroll beneath one another. Unfortunately, this system doesn't work with an pre-established window.

2.5.5 THE WINDOW AS INPUT LINE

This program makes it easy to limit the user's access to the cursor keys, and keep the user in the confines of an input line.

```
 5 REM F = 39 (40 COL.) F = 79 (80 COL.)
10 REM INPUT LINE
20 PRINT CHR$(27);"M":REM scrolling stopped
40 PRINT"NAME?";
50 OPEN 1,0
60 WINDOW PEEK(236),PEEK(235),F,PEEK(235),1
70 INPUT#1,A$
80 CLOSE 1
90 WINDOW 0,0,F,24
```

NOTE: The constant F (lines 60 & 90) should be replaced with 39 (40-col. screen) or 79 (80-col.).

Address 236 has the present column, and address 235 has the current line.

2.5.6 PRINT AT WITH WINDOWS

Many books and magazines have written about simulating PRINT AT on
the C-64. The C-128 has a command called CHAR, used to simulate
PRINT AT. But this isn't always the best method—for example, you can't
control the length of the output. Also, there might be control characters in
the string to be printed.   If you use the WINDOW, you'll come out ahead:

```
 5 REM F = 39 (40 COL.) F = 79 (80 COL.)
10 REM PRINT AT WITH WINDOWS
20 INPUT"ROW";RW
30 INPUT"COLUMN";CL
40 INPUT"LENGTH";LN
50 F=PEEK(231)
55 PRINT CHR$(27);"M":REM SCROLLING STOPPED
60 WINDOW CL,RW,CL+LN,LINE
65 PRINT"HELLO"
70 WINDOW 0,0,F,24
```

The variable F again represents the screen width. The system automatically
figures the mode out at line 50.

2.5.7 CLEARING A PARTIAL SCREEN

One part of the WINDOW command we haven't touched on is its ability to
clear window contents. You have your choice of two methods:

```
a)      10 WINDOW 10,10,20,20:PRINT"(CLR/HOME)"
b)      10 WINDOW 10,10,20,20,1
```

The uses for this are clear. We may want to erase the window, so that we can use the screen for other things. On the other hand, you may want to just clear the lower half of the 40-column screen:

```
10 WINDOW 0, 12, 39, 24, 1
20 WINDOW 0,  0, 39, 24(, 0)
```

You can, of course, use these commands in direct mode. Just type it in one line, separating the two commands with a colon (:).

2.5.8 SECURING WINDOW CONTENTS

Let's say you're in the middle of a word processing program. You've filled the entire screen, and now you want to save the text. You go to the main menu, which appears in a screen window. Good software will still retain the text under the window, and even let you go back to the text, erasing the window. The WINDOW command on the 128 doesn't do this.

Now, once the window is cleared, the contents are lost forever. What to do? We can make the window simulate a 40-column screen:

```
10    REM  SAVE SCREEN WHILE USING WINDOWS
20    GRAPHIC 0,1
30    REM  WRITE SOMETHING ON SCREEN
40    FOR I = 1024 TO 2024
50    POKE I,J
60    J = J + 1
70    IF J > 255 THEN J = 0
80    NEXT I
90    X1 = 5:   REM  DEFINE WINDOW
```

```
100    X2 = 12
110    X3 = 35
120    X4 = 22
125    REM  SAVE CONTENTS UNDER WINDOW
130    GOSUB 60000
140    REM  USE WINDOW
150    WINDOW X1,X2,X3,X4,1
160    INPUT "TEXT";A$
170    REM  RETURN SCREEN TO NORMAL
180    WINDOW 0,0,39,24,0
190    GOSUB 60090:   REM  RECALL INFO
200    GET  KEY B$
210    GRAPHIC 0,1
220    END
60000   REM  SAVE SCREEN UNDER WINDOW
60010   DIM X(350)
60020   FOR I = X2 TO X4
60030   FOR J = X1 TO X3
60040   X(Z) =  PEEK (I * 40 + J + 1024)
60050   Z = Z + 1
60060   NEXT J
60070   NEXT I
60080   RETURN
60090   REM  RECALL SCREEN
60100   Z = 0
60110   FOR I = X2 TO X4
60120   FOR J = X1 TO X3
60130   POKE I * 40 + J + 1024,X(Z)
60140   Z = Z + 1
60150   NEXT J
60160   NEXT I
60170   RETURN
```

The interesting part of this program starts at line 60000. Line 60010 defines an array called X(). The array size is dependent on the size of the windows. If you use this routine in your own programs, make sure no other arrays or variables exist with this name. If you give the coordinates for one window, you can put this value directly in the loop instead of using variables. If you use several windows you should use variables.

Like all BASIC programs, this one has a small disadvantage: It's too slow.
Here's a second version, in machine language:

```
1400 A5 E7       LDA $E7       :Right window border
1402 18          CLC
1403 E5 F6       SBC $E6       :Minus left border
1405 85 FF       STA $FF       :=length of window
1407 E6 FF       INC $FF       :Length=length+1
1409 A9 04       LDA #$04      :Screen start
140B 85 FC       STA $FC       :store
140D A2 00       LDX #$00
140F 8A          TXA
1410 E4 E5       CPX $E5       :$E5 = 1st window line?
1412 F0 0B       BEQ $141F     :YES--then $141F
1414 E8          INX
1415 18          CLC
1416 69 28       ADC #$28      :Next line
1418 90 F6       BCC $1410     :Still not all
141A E6 FC       INC $FC       :Raise high-byte pointer
141C 4C 10 14    JMP $1410
141F 18          CLC
1420 65 E6       ADC $E6       :Window start - low
1422 90 02       BCC $1426
1424 E6 FC       INC $FC       :Raise high-byte by 1
1426 85 FB       STA $FB       :Store low-byte
1428 85 FD       STA $FD       : in $FB and $FD
142A A5 FC       LDA $FC       :High-byte
142C 69 F7       ADC #$11      :17 there
142E 85 FE       STA $FE       :and in high-byte of the
1430 A0 FF       LDY #$FF      :2nd counter
1432 C8          INY
1433 AD 6B 14    LDA $146B     :Read or write?
1436 D0 1A       BNE $1452     :Write
1438 B1 FB       LDA($FB),Y    :Char. on screen
143A 91 FD       STA($FD),Y    :Store
143C C4 FF       CPY $FF       :Y-reg = length?
143E D0 F2       BNE $1432     :UNEQUAL--continue
1440 E8          INX
1441 E4 E4       CPX $E4       :X-reg = bottom edge?
1443 90 14       BCC $1459     :smaller
1445 AD 6B 14    LDA $146B     :Written or read?
1448 D0 04       BNE $144E     :Written, read next
```

```
144A EE 6B 14  INC $146B
144D 60         RTS          :Back to BASIC
144E CE 6B 14  DEC $146B
1451 60         RTS          :Return to BASIC
1452 B1 FD      LDA($FD),Y   :Char. from memory
1454 91 FB      STA($FB),Y   :written to screen
1456 4C 3C 14  JMP $143C
1459 A5 FB      LDA $FB      :Low-byte in accumulator
145B 18         CLC
145C 69 28      ADC #$28     :Next line
145E 90 04      BCC $1464    :No overflow
1460 E6 FC      INC $FC      :Raise high-byte by 1
1462 E6 FE      INC $FE      :Raise high-byte of 2nd
                              counter by 1
1464 85 FB      STA $FB      :Low-byte in 1st counter
1466 85 FD      STA $FD      :Low-byte in 2nd counter
1468 4C 30 14  JMP $1430
146B 00         BRK          :Byte for read (0)
                              or write      (1)
```

Here's the BASIC loader for the window saving routine. A sample
program has been included with the BASIC loader to demonstrate the speed
of the routine.

```
  0      GOTO 180
 10      REM   TEST PROGRAM
 20      GRAPHIC 0
 30      FOR I = 1024 TO 2023
 40      POKE I,A
 50      A = A + 1
 60      IF A > 255 THEN A = 0
 70      NEXT I
 80      WINDOW 10,10,20,20
 90      SYS 5120
100       PRINT "{CLR HOME}"
110       GET  KEY A$
120       PRINT A$;
130       IF A$ < > CHR$ (13) THEN 110
140       SYS 5120
150       WINDOW 0,0,39,24
160       GRAPHIC 0
170       END
```

```
180     REM   ROUTINE SAVE WINDOW
190     FOR I = 5120 TO 5227
200     READ A
210     S = S + A
220     POKE I,A
230     NEXT I
240     IF S <  > 16107 THEN BEGIN
250     PRINT "?ERROR IN DATA"
260     END
270     BEND
280     GOTO 10
290     DATA 165,231,24,229,230,133,255,230
300     DATA 255,169,4,133,252,162,0,138
310     DATA 228,229,240,11,232,24,105,40
320     DATA 144,246,230,252,76,16,20,24
330     DATA 101,230,144,2,230,252,133,251
340     DATA 133,253,165,252,105,17,133,254
350     DATA 160,255,200,173,107,20,208,26
360     DATA 177,251,145,253,196,255,208,242
370     DATA 228,228,232,144,20,173,107,20
380     DATA 208,4,238,107,20,96,206,107
390     DATA 20,96,177,253,145,251,76,60
400     DATA 20,165,251,24,105,40,144,4
410     DATA 230,252,230,254,133,251,133,253
420     DATA 76,48,20,0
```

The routine itself begins at line 180. The first section contains the sample
program. The window in which you read and write text must always be
active.

2.5.9 SIMULATING SEVERAL WINDOWS

We can simulate a number of windows with the help of the BASIC program
in Chapter 2.5.8:

```
10      REM  SAVE WINDOW CONTENTS
15      DIM X(40,30)
20      GRAPHIC 0,1
30      REM  FILL SCREEN WITH TEXT
40      FOR I = 1024 TO 2024
50      POKE I,J
60      J = J + 1
70      IF J > 255 THEN J = 0
80      NEXT I
85      REM  PUT 40 WINDOWS ON SCREEN
90      FOR K = 0 TO 39
100     X1 =  INT ( RND (1) * 25) + 5
110     X2 =  INT ( RND (1) * 14) + 3
115     REM  SAVE CONTENTS UNDER WINDOW
120     GOSUB 60000
130     WINDOW X1,X2,X1 + 4,X2 + 3
140     FOR W = 1 TO 20:  REM  PRINT #'S IN WINDOW
150     PRINT  CHR$ (K + 48);
160     NEXT W
165     NEXT K
170     REM  TAKE OFF WINDOWS ON SCREEN
180     FOR K = 39 TO 0 STEP  - 1
190     X1 = X(K,29)
200     X2 = X(K,30)
210     WINDOW X1,X2,X1 + 4,X2 + 3
215     REM  REPLACE CONTENTS
220     GOSUB 60090
230     NEXT K
240     GET  KEY A$
250     GRAPHIC 0,1
260     END
60000 REM  MEMORIZE CONTENTS UNDER WINDOW
60010 Z = 0
60020 FOR I = X2 TO X2 + 3
```

```
60030 FOR J = X1 TO X1 + 4
60040 X(K,Z) =   PEEK (I * 40 + J + 1024)
60050 Z = Z + 1
60060 NEXT J
60070 NEXT I
60074 X(K,29) = X1
60076 X(K,30) = X2
60080 RETURN
60090 REM   RECALL CONTENTS
60100 Z = 0
60110 FOR I = X2 TO X2 + 3
60120 FOR J = X1 TO X1 + 4
60130 POKE I * 40 + J + 1024,X(K,Z)
60140 Z = Z + 1
60150 NEXT J
60160 NEXT I
60170 RETURN
```

First, a screen is displayed, then 40 windows are produced, then the windows are cleared. The final result is the starting screen.

This program shows you how to use multiple windows. Using multiple windows in your own programs entails writing individual routines for each window.

The program works with 40 windows, the largest number possible in C-128 variable memory. The array X() uses 40 * 1004 bytes (40 refers to the number of windows, of course). If you use fewer in your program, decrease the number proportionately.

It's possible to extend a window over the entire screen. This would require 1000 bytes for screen contents, and four for window coordinates, resulting in 1004. Again, a smaller window requires a smaller number.

2.6 SPRITE HANDLING

Another indicator of BASIC 7.0's versatility is its sprite handling commands. The sprite generating and editing features make sprite work very easy (as opposed to the C-64, where sprite handling is made very difficult with BASIC 2.0).

It goes without saying that games make up the majority of sprite applications. You can also use sprites instead of regular characters (see Chapter 3.5). The next program was designed for just that; it copies the character of your choice into the sprite editor, where you can make your own lettering (eight sprites are available).

```
  5    REM   2.6A
 10    REM   CHAR. COPIER TO SPRITE
 20    INPUT "WHICH SPRITE";S
 30    IF S < 1 OR S > 8 THEN 20
 40    INPUT "COL   (0-13) ";Z
 50    IF Z < 0 OR Z > 13 THEN 40
 60    INPUT "ROW    (0-2) ";Y
 70    IF Y < 0 OR Y > 2 THEN 60
 80    REM   ERASE SPRITE
 90    FOR I = 0 TO 62
100    B$ = B$ +  CHR$ (0)
110    NEXT I
120    SPRSAV B$,S
130    IF Z = 0 AND Y = 0 THEN 170
140    FOR I = 1 TO Z * 3 + Y
150    A$ = A$ +  CHR$ (0)
160    NEXT I
170    INPUT "INPUT CHAR. CODE ";C
180    FOR I = C * 8 TO C * 8 + 7
190    A = 0
200    FOR J = 0 TO 7
210    BANK 14
220    F =  PEEK (53248 + I)
```

```
230    IF (F AND 2 ^ J) = 2 ^ J THEN A = A + 2 ^ J
240    NEXT J
250    A$ = A$ +  CHR$ (A) +  CHR$ (0) +  CHR$ (0)
260    NEXT I
270    SPRSAV A$,S
280    REM  SPRITE IMAGE GENERATOR
290    POKE 842,48 + S
300    POKE 843,13
310    POKE 208,2
320    SPRDEF
```

You need to enter the screen code of the character you want. After you've
done that, the system copies the character into the SPRDEF mode, where
you have sprite commands at your fingertips. Then again, there isn't a
whole lot you can do with a character built within an 8X8 matrix; the
majority of the sprite field is left unused. The second program doubles the
size of the sprites, allowing you to use multicolor mode, and, for instance,
make a sprite with a shadow trailing behind it.

```
10     REM  DOUBLE SIZE CHAR COPY TO SPRITE
20     INPUT "WHICH SPRITE";T
30     IF T < 1 OR T > 8 THEN 20
40     INPUT "COL.  (0-5) ";Z
50     IF Z < 0 OR Z > 5 THEN 40
60     INPUT "ROW    (0-1) ";Y
70     IF Y < 0 OR Y > 1 THEN 60
80     REM  SPRITE ERASE
90     FOR I = 0 TO 62
100    B$ = B$ +  CHR$ (0)
110    NEXT I
120    SPRSAV B$,T
130    IF Z = 0 AND Y = 0 THEN 170
140    FOR I = 1 TO Z * 3 + Y
150    A$ = A$ +  CHR$ (0)
160    NEXT I
170    INPUT "INPUT CHAR CODE   ";S
175    REM  CHAR COPIER
180    FOR I = S * 8 TO S * 8 + 7
190    A(0) = 0
```

```
200    A(1) = 0
210    FOR J = 0 TO 3
220    FOR Q = 0 TO 1
230    BANK 14
240    F =  PEEK (53248 + I)
250    IF (F AND 2 ^ (J + Q * 3)) = 2 ^ (J + Q * 3)
       THEN A(Q) =A(Q) + 2 ^ (J * 2) + 2 ^ (J * 2+1)
260    NEXT Q
270    NEXT J
280    A$ = A$ + CHR$ (A(1)) + CHR$ (A(0)) +CHR$ (0)
290    A$ = A$ + CHR$ (A(1)) + CHR$ (A(0)) +CHR$ (0)
300    NEXT I
310    SPRSAV A$,T
320    REM  ACTIVATE SPRITE IMAGE GENERATOR
330    POKE 842,48 + T
340    POKE 843,13
350    POKE 208,2
360    SPRDEF
```

2.6.1 DESIGN IN LISTING

One thing is a little puzzling about sprites: where are the sprite contents going to be stored? We've designed the two following programs to fix that problem. The first program reads DATA statements to form a sprite. That is, there's no DATA per se, but rather strings. They're faster and simpler for the computer to handle, and changes are easily made on these sprites. Like most of the BASIC listings, this one, too, is slow; but it beats buying a program.

```
10     REM  DESIGN IMAGE LISTING 1
20     INPUT "HOW MANY SPRITES";S
30     POKE 53296,1 : REM SET FAST MODE
40     FOR T = 1 TO S:  PRINT "READING IN SPRITE #"T
50     A$ = ""
```

```
60      FOR G = 0 TO 20
70      READ B$
80      IF  LEN (B$) < 24 THEN B$ = B$ + ".": GOTO 80
90      FOR I = 0 TO 2
100     A = 0
110     FOR J = 0 TO 7
120     IF MID$ (B$,I*8+J+1,1) ="*" THEN A =A+2^(7-J)
130     NEXT J
140     A$ = A$ +  CHR$ (A)
150     NEXT I
160     NEXT G
170     SPRSAV A$,T
180     SPRITE T,1,T,1,1,1,0
190     MOVSPR T,T * 10#T
200     NEXT T
210     POKE 53296,0
1000    REM   0123456789012345678890123
1010    DATA ********
1020    DATA ********
1030    DATA .******
1040    DATA ..******
1050    DATA ...******
1060    DATA ....******
1070    DATA ....***********
1080    DATA ....*************
1090    DATA ......****************
1100    DATA ......*****************
1110    DATA .......******************
1120    DATA ......******************
1130    DATA .....*****************
1140    DATA ....*************
1150    DATA ....************
1160    DATA ....******
1170    DATA ...******
1180    DATA ..******
1190    DATA .******
1200    DATA ********
1210    DATA ********
1220    REM   0123456789012345678890123
```

As you can see from the listing, a set bit in a sprite is shown as an asterisk,
and an unset bit a period.

While the data is being read in, the clock frequency is doubled (FAST), which increases execution time, but turns off the 40-column screen. When the routine finishes, the screen returns to normal, and a sprite is displayed on the screen.

Not every program uses this method of reading sprites as DATA statements, so we wrote the second program in this chapter, which automatically cranks out DATA statements.

```
10    REM  DESIGN IMAGE LISTING 2
20    INPUT "HOW MANY SPRITES";S
30    FOR T = 1 TO S
40    FOR G = 0 TO 62 STEP 3
50    B$ = ""
60    FOR I = 0 TO 2
70    FOR J = 7 TO 0 STEP  - 1
80    IF (PEEK(3520+G+I+T*64) AND 2^J) = 2^J THEN
      B$ = B$ + "*":  ELSE B$ = B$ + "."
90    NEXT J
100   NEXT I
110   PRINT  STR$ (10000 + G + 100 * T);" DATA";B$
120   PRINT "GOTO 170{CRSR UP}{CRSR UP}{CRSR UP}";:
      REM  3*CURSOR ^
130   POKE 842,13
140   POKE 843,13
150   POKE 208,2
160   END
170   NEXT G
180   NEXT T
190   REM  DATA AT 10100-
```

Once the routine is done, remove the old DATA lines with the DELETE command.

2.6.2 COMFORTABLE SPRITE EDITING

After defining a sprite, you might like to alter it. For example, you've designed a spaceship, and you discover that it wasn't that great a design. Instead of redoing it completely, just run it through this program. Ah, but there's more—it can also expand the sprite in two axis *and* rotate the sprite.

```
10    REM   ************** SPRITE-HANDLING
20    DIM B(600)
30    DIM A(62)
40    REM   ************** MENU
50    INPUT "COLOR 1";F
60    INPUT "COLOR 2";D
70    INPUT "COLOR 3";E
80    SPRCOLOR D,E
90    PRINT "1 :   VERTICAL MIRROR"
100   PRINT "2 :   HORIZONTAL MIRROR"
110   PRINT "3 :   ROTATE 180 DEG."
120   PRINT "4 :   DISPLAY SPRITE"
130   PRINT "5 :   INVERT"
140   PRINT "6 :   ROTATE 90 DEG."
150   PRINT "7 :   ROTATE 270 DEG."
160   INPUT "COMMAND";B
165   IF B = 0 THEN   END
170   IF B < 1 OR B > 7 THEN   GOTO 10
180   INPUT "SPRITE-NUMBER ";S
190   IF S < 1 OR S > 9 THEN   GOTO 180
200   IF B<5 THEN INPUT"MULTICOLOR (ON=1/OFF=0)  ";M
210   :   ELSE M = 0
220   POKE 53296,1
230   IF B > 3 THEN 270
240   FOR I = 0 TO 62
250   A(I) =   PEEK (3520 + S * 64 + I)
260   NEXT I
270   ON B GOSUB 360,430,560,420,600,830,650
280   REM   ****** SPRITE VERTICAL MIRROR
290   POKE 53296,0
300   GRAPHIC 0,1
```

```
300   GRAPHIC 0,1
310   SPRITE S,1,F,1,1,1,M
320   MOVSPR S,100,100
330   GET  KEY A$
340   SPRITE S,0
350   GOTO 90
360   REM  *********** VERTICAL MIRROR
370   FOR I = 0 TO 60 STEP 3
380   FOR J = 0 TO 2
390   POKE 3520 + S * 64 + I + J,A(60 - I + J)
400   NEXT J
410   NEXT I
420   RETURN
430   REM  *********** HORIZONTAL MIRROR
440   FOR I = 0 TO 60 STEP 3
450   FOR J = 0 TO 2
460   W = 0
470   FOR X = M TO 7 STEP M + 1
480   IF (A(I+2-J) AND 2^X) =2^X THEN W = W+2^(7-X)
490   IF M =1 AND (A(I +2-J) AND 2^(X-1)) = 2^(X-1)
      THEN W = W+2^(7-(X-1))
500   NEXT X
510   A(I + 2 - J) = W
520   POKE 3520 + S * 64 + I + J,A(I + 2 - J)
530   NEXT J
540   NEXT I
550   RETURN
560   REM  ********* ROTATE 180 DEG.
570   GOSUB 360
580   B = 2
590   GOTO 240
600   REM  ************** INVERT
610   FOR I = 0 TO 62
620   POKE3520+S*64+I,255AND(-PEEK(3520+S*64+I)-1)
630   NEXT I
640   RETURN
650   REM  ********* ROTATE 270 DEG.
660   FOR I = 0 TO 20
670   FOR J = 0 TO 2
680   FOR G = 0 TO 7
690   B((I*3+J)*8+7-G) = (PEEK(3520+S*64+I*3+J)
      AND 2^G)/2^G
700   NEXT G
```

```
710   POKE 3520 + S * 64 + I * 3 + J,0
720   NEXT J
730   NEXT I
740   FOR I = 0 TO 2
750   FOR J = 0 TO 20
760   FOR G = 0 TO 7
770   IF B(I * 192 + J + (7 - G) * 24) = 0 THEN 790
780   POKE 3520+S*64+I+(20-J)*3,
      PEEK (3520+S*64+I+(20-J)*3) OR 2^G
790   NEXT G
800   NEXT J
810   NEXT I
820   RETURN
830   REM   ********** ROTATE 90 DEG.
840   GOSUB 650
850   B = 2
860   GOTO 240
```

During the recalculation, the 40-character screen flickers a lot, which tells us that the "high speed" mode (FAST) is on again. The system will return to normal when the program is finished, and the new sprite is displayed on the screen. Pressing any key will return you to the menu.

Here's a quick rundown of the functions:

1. Mirroring

   The sprite will be turned upside-down. The point DATA will *not* be inverted.

2. Mirroring by axis.

   Hard to describe; splits inverted sprite.

3. Turn 180 Degrees

   Self-explanatory.

4. Display Sprite

   This lets you see the sprite at any time.

5. Reverse

   Not to be confused with mirroring -- the sprite comes up as a
   "negative" (i.e., reverse video). Multicolor mode is not in
   this program, but you can still use the sprite in that mode
   later.

6. Turn 90 Degrees

   Self-explanatory.

7. Turn 270 Degrees

   Self-explanatory.

C. Copy sprite

   Self-explanatory.

Final note: Pressing "C" copies the original sprite, so you have a backup if
you destroy your original during experimentation.

CHAPTER 3

USEFUL PROGRAMS

The next few pages contain programs designed to help you in your everyday computing. We've made them fairly simple, so you can make any changes appropriate to your work. Have fun!

3.1 ERROR HANDLING

You've probably heard this maxim before: "The first step is always the hardest." And no doubt you've heard this quote, attributed to a guy named Murphy: "If something *can* go wrong, it *will*." Both these sayings seem to apply directly to the programmer. In the initial phases of programming, we say to ourselves, "What are all these error messages?" The more advanced programmer generally recognizes at least some of the error messages, but he still ends up doing a lot of debugging.

Some BASIC versions have a HELP function, and the C-128 is no exception. This function finds the errant line, and shows the error in reverse video (40-column mode) or underscoring (80-columns). You can also use the command within a BASIC program.

Although the C-128 has no ON ERROR GOTO command, it does have a TRAP command. Type the command, followed by a line number, and an error will cause the system to jump to that line.

Next, we have the ERR$ variable. The variable ER stores the numbers of error, and PRINT ERR$(ER) prints the corresponding error messages. Finally, there's the variable EL, which contains the line number of the "bad" line.

If the program stops due to a TRAP command, there are three possible methods of continuing the program, all by means of the RESUME command. Typing in RESUME alone causes the computer to continue at the line where the error occurred. Giving a line number with RESUME causes the program to continue from the line specified. Finally, you can type in NEXT after RESUME; then the system starts from the line after the "bad" line.

If you want to watch your program step-by-step, if only to see what the errors are doing, you have TRON and TROFF at hand. These control the TRACE function.

Now for a some applications using these commands:

a) For Beginners

Type in this program:

```
10  TRAP 1000
20  :
30  PRINT:PRIND: REM PRIND NOT PRINT
40  PRINT CHR$(147)"(C) 1985 BY WERNER
50  FOR T=1 TO 10:PRINT:NEXT Y
60  PRINT"OK"
70  END
80  :
1000  REM ERROR JMP
```

```
1030 PRINT"(CRSR DOWN)(CYAN)'G'O ON OR 'E'ND?"
1040 GET KEY A$
1050 IF A$="E" THEN END
1060 IF A$="G" THEN RESUME NEXT
1070 GOTO 1040
```

The program jumps to line 1000 whenever it runs into an error (e.g., at line 30) as a result of the TRAP command at line 10. The error trap routine gives you the type of error and the line number at which it occurred. That's all the routine does; it's up to you to find the error (HELP key) and correct it.

A tip for machine language programmers: You can develop an "error statement" program for machine language errors. The vector for printing BASIC errors is at locations $0300/$0301, and the error number is given in the X-register. The X-register presents the value $80 when no errors exist. On the next page are the errors and their values:

NUMBER (hex)	:	NUMBER (dec):	ERROR
$01	:	1	:TOO MANY FILES
$02	:	2	:FILE OPEN
$03	:	3	:FILE NOT OPEN
$04	:	4	:FILE NOT FOUND
$05	:	5	:DEVICE NOT PRESENT
$06	:	6	:NOT INPUT FILE
$07	:	7	:NOT OUTPUT FILE
$08	:	8	:MISSING FILENAME
$09	:	9	:ILLEGAL DEVICE NUMBER
$0A	:	10	:NEXT WITHOUT FOR
$0B	:	11	:SYNTAX
$0C	:	12	:RETURN WITHOUT GOSUB
$0D	:	13	:OUT OF DATA
$0E	:	14	:ILLEGAL QUANTITY
$0F	:	15	:OVERFLOW
$10	:	16	:OUT OF MEMORY
$11	:	17	:UNDEF'D STATEMENT
$12	:	18	:BAD SUBSCRIPT
$13	:	19	:REDIM'D ARRAY
$14	:	20	:DIVISION BY ZERO
$15	:	21	:ILLEGAL DIRECT
$16	:	22	:TYPE MISMATCH
$17	:	23	:STRING TOO LONG
$18	:	24	:FILE DATA
$19	:	25	:FORMULA TOO COMPLEX
$1A	:	26	:CAN'T CONTINUE
$1B	:	27	:UNDEF'D FUNCTION
$1C	:	28	:VERIFY
$1D	:	29	:LOAD
$1E	:	30	:BREAK
$1F	:	31	:CAN'T RESUME
$20	:	32	:LOOP NOT FOUND
$21	:	33	:LOOP WITHOUT DO
$22	:	34	:DIRECT MODE ONLY
$23	:	35	:NO GRAPHICS AREA
$24	:	36	:BAD DISK
$25	:	37	:BEND NOT FOUND
$26	:	38	:LINE NUMBER TOO LARGE
$27	:	39	:UNRESOLVED REFERENCE
$28	:	40	:UNIMPLEMENTED COMMAND
$29	:	41	:FILE READ

2. The Use of RESUME

Typing RESUME without a line number or NEXT can result in an endless loop, which probably wasn't what the designers of BASIC 7.0 had in mind. Try this program out:

```
1       TRAP 1000
10      CATALOG
20      END
1000    IF ER=5 THEN PRINT CHR$(19);"PLEASE TURN
        DISK DRIVE ON": RESUME
1010    END
```

Turn your disk drive off and run the program, which looks for the disk directory. Since the drive is off, the system responds with "DEVICE NOT PRESENT" and jumps to line 1000. Seeing error number 5, the program asks you to switch the disk drive on. The RESUME command causes the program to continue displaying this message until the drive is finally turned on.

Now for a sample of RESUME with a line number:

```
1       TRAP 1000
10      INPUT"FILENAME";NA$
20      INPUT"DEVICE NUMBER";DV
30      LOAD NA$,DV
40      END
1000    IF ER=4 THEN PRINT"THERE IS NO SUCH
        FILENAME":RESUME 10
1010    IF ER=5 THEN PRINT"PLEASE TURN DISK DRIVE
        ON":RESUME
1020    IF ER=8 THEN PRINT"PLEASE GIVE ME A
        FILENAME":RESUME 10
1030    IF ER=9 THEN PRINT"PICK A DEVICE NR FROM
        8 - 15": RESUME 20
1040    END
```

Essentially, this little routine can make a program "foolproof". That is, it won't stop if you give it a bad filename, have your disk drive turned off, press <RETURN> on the filename prompt, or give it a non-disk device address. And, it will tell you what the problem is, in simple English.

3.2 *LISTER* - A LISTING UTILITY

You've just spent your last dollar on a computer magazine. You run home, switch on the computer, and start typing in page upon page of program listing. Wait a minute; there's something wrong here. The problem is, as in so many cases, the printout in the magazine is from a Commodore printer. You know what that means: Unreadable control characters -- what's this reversed heart? And this reverse-video cross? Eventually you give up and either buy the companion disk—or just stop buying the magazine.

Some computer magazines have heard the cries of their readers. These publishers use a special listing technique to alter the program listing so that, instead of control characters, a descriptive term or abbreviation appear (e.g., "{CLR}" or "{5 DOWN}") in the listing.

There's an advantage to this. It increases the marketability of the magazine. It's a lot easier for a user to just punch CRSR DOWN from the listing, rather than look at the graphic symbol, flip through the manual, figure out what that symbol actually does, then type it in. On the other hand, there's a greater frustration that isn't cured. How many spaces do I put here? Are there 39 or 40 (or 38)? How many CRSR DOWNs? And so on....

Our *LISTER* fixes that problem: Any spaces and control characters in quotes and in number will be printed out with their amounts. Plus, each command will be separated by a space. This can be a godsend to the beginner. It's a lot easier to read;

```
FOR ES = 1 TO P: W = PEEK (ES) AND NOT 5 OR 8
```

than it is to read:

```
FORES=1TOP:W=PEEK(ES)ANDNOT5OR8.
```

The design of the printout is familiar to those of you who are also Apple users: commands are indented, variables are not.

Now for the program: Type it in and SAVE it with the name *LISTER* before trying it out.

```
1       REM  LISTING OF LISTER CHAPTER 3.2.A
5       PRINT "{CLR HOME}PLEASE WAIT..."
10      DIM TK$(255),FE$(29),CE$(8),SZ$(159)
20      FOR Z = 0 TO 125: READ WE$,A$: TK$( DEC
        (WE$)) = A$:   NEXT Z
22      FOR Z = 0 TO 27:  READ WE$,A$: FE$( DEC
        (WE$)) = A$:   NEXT Z
24      FOR Z = 0 TO 7:   READ WE$,A$: CE$( DEC (WE$))
        = A$:   NEXT Z
26      FOR Z = 0 TO 25:  READ WE$,A$: SZ$( DEC
        (WE$)) = A$:   NEXT Z
30      AN = 7168
40      PRINT "{CLR HOME}'S'CREEN OR 'P'RINTER?"
42      DR = 0:  GET  KEY A$:  IF A$ = "D" THEN DR =
        1:  GOTO 50
44      IF A$ <  > "B" THEN 40
50      PRINT "{CRSR DOWN}'U'PPEROR'L'OWERCASE?"
```

```
52    GET  KEY A$:   IF A$ = "L" THEN   PRINT
      CHR$ (14):   GOTO 60
54    IF A$ <  > "U" THEN   PRINT "{CRSR UP}";:
      GOTO 50
60    INPUT "{LINE FEED}NAME OF THE PROGRAM";NA$
70    IF DR THEN   CLOSE 4:   OPEN 4,4,0
72    PRINT :   PRINT NA$:   PRINT
73    IF DR THEN   PRINT# 4:   PRINT# 4,NA$: PRINT# 4
100   FL = 0: AN = AN + 3
102   LO = PEEK (AN): AN = AN + 1: HI = PEEK (AN):
      ZE = LO + 256 * HI
105   PRINT ZE;" ";
106   IF DR THEN   PRINT# 4,ZE;" ";
110   AN = AN + 1
115   WE =   PEEK (AN):   IF WE = 0 THEN 1000
120   IF WE = 32 THEN 2000
122   IF WE = 34 THEN 7000
123   IF WE = 58 THEN 8000
125   IF WE =   DEC ("FE") THEN 3000
130   IF WE =   DEC ("CE") THEN 4000
135   IF FF THEN 6000
140   GOTO 5000
999   :
1000 REM   NEW LINE
1009 IF DR THEN   PRINT# 4
1010 PRINT : IF PEEK (AN + 1) = 0 AND PEEK (AN +
      2) = 0 THEN   CLOSE 4:   END
1020 GOTO 100
1999 :
2000 REM   EMPTY LINE
2010 IF FF THEN 6030
2020 IF FL THEN   PRINT " ";
2021 IF DR AND FL THEN   PRINT# 4," ";
2030 GOTO 110
2999 :
3000 REM   $FE
3010 AN = AN + 1: WE =   PEEK (AN)
3020 PRINT FE$(WE);" ";
3021 IF DR THEN   PRINT# 4,FE$(WE);" ";
3030 GOTO 110
3999 :
4000 REM   $CE
4010 AN = AN + 1: WE =   PEEK (AN)
```

```
4020 PRINT CE$(WE);" ";
4021 IF DR THEN  PRINT# 4,CE$(WE);" ";
4030 GOTO 110
4999 :
5000 REM  BEGINNING OF STRING
5005 IF WE = 143 THEN FL = 1
5010 IF TK$(WE) < > "" THEN 5040
5020 PRINT  CHR$ (WE);
5021 IF DR THEN  PRINT# 4, CHR$ (WE);
5030 GOTO 110
5040 PRINT " ";TK$(WE);" ";
5041 IF DR THEN  PRINT# 4," ";TK$(WE);" ";
5050 GOTO 110
5999 :
6000 REM  INNER PART OF STRINGS
6005 IF WE < > 255 THEN 6010
6006 PRINT "π";
6007 IF DR THEN  PRINT# 4,"π";
6008 GOTO 110
6010 IF SZ$(WE) < > "" THEN 6030
6020 PRINT  CHR$ (WE);
6021 IF DR THEN  PRINT# 4, CHR$ (WE);
6025 GOTO 110
6030 ZA = 1
6040 IF  PEEK (AN + 1) < > WE THEN 6060
6050 AN = AN + 1: ZA = ZA + 1:  GOTO 6040
6060 PRINT  CHR$ (18);"[";SZ$(WE); STR$ (ZA);"]";
     CHR$ (146);
6061 IF DR THEN  PRINT# 4," [";SZ$(WE); STR$
     (ZA);"] ";
6070 GOTO 110
6999 :
7000 REM  QUOTATION MARK
7010 FF = XOR (FF,255)
7020 PRINT  CHR$ (34);:  POKE 244,0
7021 IF DR THEN  PRINT# 4, CHR$ (34);
7030 GOTO 110
7999 :
8000 REM  COLON
8010 PRINT  CHR$ (58);" ";
8011 IF DR THEN  PRINT# 4, CHR$ (58);" ";
8020 GOTO 110
9999 :
```

```
10000 DATA "80","END","81","FOR","82","NEXT",
      "83","DATA","84","INPUT#"
10010 DATA "85","INPUT","86","DIM","87","READ",
      "88","LET","89","GOTO"
10020 DATA "8A","RUN","8B","IF","8C","RESTORE",
      "8D","GOSUB","8E","RETURN"
10030 DATA "8F","REM","90","STOP","91","ON",
      "92","WAIT","93","LOAD","94","SAVE"
10040 DATA "95","VERIFY","96","DEF","97","POKE",
      "98","PRINT#","99","PRINT"
10050 DATA "9A","CONT","9B","LIST","9C","CLR",
      "9D","CMD","9E","SYS","9F","OPEN"
10060 DATA "A0","CLOSE","A1","GET","A2","NEW",
      "A3","TAB(","A4","TO","A5","FN"
10070 DATA "A6","SPC(","A7","THEN","A8","NOT",
      "A9","STEP","AA","+","AB","-"
10080 DATA "AC","*","AD","/","AE","^","AF","AND",
      "B0","OR","B1",">","B2","="
10090 DATA "B3","<","B4","SGN","B5","INT",
      "B6","ABS","B7","USR","B8","FRE"
10100 DATA "B9","POS","BA","SQR","BB","RND",
      "BC","LOG","BD","EXP","BE","COS"
10110 DATA "BF","SIN","C0","TAN","C1","ATN",
      "C2","PEEK","C3","LEN","C4","STR$"
10120 DATA "C5","VAL","C6","ASC","C7","CHR$",
      "C8","LEFT$","C9","RIGHT$"
10130 DATA "CA","MID$","CB","GO","CC","RGR",
      "CD","RCLR","CF","JOY","D0","RDOT"
10140 DATA "D1","DEC","D2","HEX$","D3","ERR$",
      "D4","INSTR","D5","ELSE"
10150 DATA "D6","RESUME","D7","TRAP","D8","TRON",
      "D9","TROFF","DA","SOUND"
10160 DATA "DB","VOL","DC","AUTO","DD","PUDEF",
      "DE","GRAPHIC","DF","PAINT"
10170 DATA "E0","CHAR","E1","BOX","E2","CIRCLE",
      "E3","GSHAPE","E4","SSHAPE"
10180 DATA "E5","DRAW","E6","LOCATE","E7","COLOR",
      "E8","SCNCLR","E9","SCALE"
10190 DATA "EA","HELP","EB","DO","EC","LOOP",
      "ED","EXIT","EE","DIRECTORY"
10200 DATA "EF","DSAVE","F0","DLOAD","F1",
      "HEADER","F2","SCRATCH"
```

```
10210 DATA "F3","COLLECT","F4","COPY","F5",
      "RENAME","F6","BACKUP","F7","DELETE"
10220 DATA "F8","RENUMBER","F9","KEY","FA",
      "MONITOR","FB","USING","FC","WHILE"
10230 DATA "FD","UNTIL","FF","π"
11000 DATA "02","BANK","03","FILTER","04",
      "PLAY","05","TEMPO","06","MOVSPR"
11010 DATA "07","SPRITE","08","SPRCOLOR",
      "09","RREG","0A","ENVELOPE"
11020 DATA "0B","SLEEP","0C","CATALOG","0D",
      "DOPEN","0E","APPEND","0F","DCLOSE"
11030 DATA "10","BSAVE","11","BLOAD","12",
      "RECORD","13","CONCAT","14","DVERIFY"
11040 DATA "15","DCLEAR","16","SPRSAV","17",
      "COLLISION","18","BEGIN"
11050 DATA "19","BEND","1A","WINDOW","1B",
      "BOOT","1C","WIDTH","1D","SPRDEF"
12000 DATA "00","RWINDOW","02","POT","03","BUMP",
      "04","PEN","05","RSPPOS"
12010 DATA "06","RSPRITE","07","RSPCOLOR",
      "08","XOR"
13000 DATA "03","RUN STOP","05","WHT",
      "0A","LINE FEED","11","CRSR DOWN"
13010 DATA "12","RVS ON","13","HOME",
      "1C","RED","1D","CRSR RIGHT","1E","GRN"
13020 DATA "1F","BLU","20","SPACE","81","ORNG",
      "90","BLK","91","CRSR UP"
13030 DATA "92","RVS OFF","93","CLR HOME",
      "95","BRN","96","L RED"
13040 DATA "97","D GRY","98","M GRY","99","L GRN",
      "9A","L BLU"
13050 DATA "9B","L GRY","9C","PUR",
      "9D","CRSR LEFT","9E","YEL","9F","CYN"
```

Now RUN it. After a short wait, you'll be asked for some input parameters. For the moment, press "S" for screen and "U" for uppercase. Then enter "*LISTER*". This isn't for loading from disk—just a heading for the listing. If you typed the program in correctly, the system will print "*LISTER*" on the screen and the program will be listed to the screen;

control characters should be spelled out in reverse on the screen. Next, switch on your printer and run the program again to get a hardcopy listing of the program.

When you want to use this program to print other listings, you'll need to do the following:

A) Move the start of BASIC - set pointers $2D (45) and $2E (46) higher than the length of the program to be listed and place a zero in the first location of the new start of BASIC. Here are the commands we used:

```
POKE  46, 192 : POKE 49152, 0: NEW
```

This moves the start of BASIC to $C000. Try the FRE(0) function after typing in these commands, less than 16K is free. This is more than enough memory to run our converter program.

B) LOAD the listing converter program with LOAD *"LISTER"*, 8. The { ,8 } is important! This command loads the listing converter program into memory at the new start of BASIC.

C) Load in the program you wish listed with the command LOAD "program-name" ,8,1. The { ,8,1 } is very important here. This command loads the program into memory at the normal start of BASIC. Because you have moved the start of BASIC the *LISTER* program is not overwritten. LIST the program to be sure.

D) RUN the *LISTER* to get a formatted listing.

You could revise the *LISTER* program so that it reads the program directly from disk, which would save the trouble of moving the start-of-BASIC. We tried that with the program listings in this book. They were transferred to this book with a modified version of the above program that used the RS-232 adapter to send the listing to another computer. The memory resident version is much faster.

A few things you should know about the memory resident *LISTER*. It looks at and interprets every byte from the normal start of BASIC. If it finds a zero, it checks the next few bytes; a set of three zeroes indicates the end of the program, and the *LISTER* halts. Every character is tested to see if it is a token; if not, the character is tested for whether it is within quotes or not. Tokens are printed out as commands. Strings with color graphic symbols will have their colors "spelled out".

Here are a few of the variables used in the program:

DR: If DR=0, the listing goes to the screen only; if DR=1, then it's sent to the printer and the screen.

FL: If equal to 1, the characters are placed after a REM.

AN: Address of bytes read.

WE: Contents of the above address.

FF: If 0, the byte is not in quotes; 1, the byte is a string (within quotes).

ZA: Counter -- counts number of consecutive characters (lines 6040-6070). Determines number of spaces in a string.

TK$(255): Contains command strings of individual tokens.

FE$(29): Contains command strings which have a value of $FE in the first byte.

CE$(8):　　Same as FE$, but for commands beginning with $CE.

SZ$(159):　Graphic character codes are held here.

3.3 OLD

What do you do if you accidentally type NEW while a program you haven't saved is in memory? No more program, right? Wrong. All is not lost. You'll remember the programs running around for the C-64 known by various titles (OLD or UNNEW); these programs renewed the bytes at the start of a program that had been zeroed out by an errant NEW command. These two bytes point to the next line number of a program (the address of the next line number, to be more specific). In addition to finding and resetting the starting address, the start-of-variables must be reset as well before the program can be completely recovered.

These OLD routines are fairly long and inaccurate most of the time. There's a much easier way of going about it:

a)　Put any number ($\neq 0$) into the two skipped bytes. This works best when you use the high-byte of start-of-BASIC.

b)　Next, call the BASIC interpreter routine that restores the BASIC program lines, and is usually used for inserting program lines in editing. It changes all the vectors (line links) and recalculates appropriately. The link to the first program line, which were zeroes a moment ago, are re-inserted into memory, and recalculated.

C)　Start of variables is set at the end of the program.

This process is much simpler on the C-128: Step c) can be eliminated, since variables are stored in Bank 1, and don't collide with Bank 0. You can activate OLD by doing this:

```
POKE PEEK(45)+256*PEEK(46)+1,28:SYS DEC("4F4F")
```

Addresses 45/46 point to start-of-BASIC. Calling this routine restores the pointers. This is what it looks like in machine language.

```
0B00 A0 01        LDY #$01        ;Offset 1
0B02 A9 1C        LDA #$1C        ;28 for BASIC RAM start
0B04 91 2D        STA ($2D),Y     ;and in link high-byte
0B06 20 4F 4F     JSR $4F4F       ;Determine links
0B09 60           RTS             ;End
```

You can put the routine anywhere in memory, not just at $0B00.

OLD also works if you've changed the BASIC pointers (say, for the conversion program in chapter 3.2). Not even a RESET can outsmart this program.

There is one exception -- when start-of-BASIC is moved up *and* a RESET is executed; then OLD goes for the normal starting address of BASIC, and won't find it there. If you know where the starting address is, just change the parameters accordingly, and you should be able to recover the program.

3.4 A LITTLE MUSIC ON THE SIDE....

Some folks like music while they're typing. That's great, unless there's no radio or stereo nearby, and most of us aren't born singers. Hiring an in-house pianist can be expensive, and typewriters don't make music. The C-128, however, CAN make music. The next program actually plays a piece of music while you're working with the computer. You can listen through your television or monitor, or run it through your stereo, etc.

The BASIC loader is a long one; the main reason is the 99-note tune within. To play a note, the SID chip needs two numbers per note (high-byte/low-byte) and a duration, which gives us a total of 297 DATA elements. You'll find this DATA at the end of the program.

```
0          REM   IRQ MUSIC
10         FOR I = 5120 TO 5198
20         READ A
30         POKE I,A
40         S = S + A
50         NEXT I
60         IF S <> 8891 THEN PRINT "?ERROR IN DATA":END
70         DATA 120,169,22,141,20,3,169,20
80         DATA 141,21,3,88,160,0
90         DATA 140,243,20,200,140,241,20,96
100        DATA 206,241,20,208,49,72,141,0
110        DATA 255,141,18,212,138,72,174,243,20
120        DATA 189,0,21,141,14,212,189,0
130        DATA 22,141,15,212,189,0,23,141
140        DATA 241,20,169,65,141,18,212,232
150        DATA 56,224,99,144,2,162,0,142
160        DATA 243,20,104,170,104,76,101,250
170        BANK 15
180        POKE 54296,15
190        POKE 54288,255
200        POKE 54289,0
```

```
210      POKE 54291,15
220      POKE 54292,0
230      N = 99:   REM   99 NOTES
240      FOR I = 0 TO N - 1
250      READ A
260      POKE 5376 + I,A
270      READ A
280      POKE 5632 + I,A
290      READ A
300      POKE 5888 + I,A
310      NEXT I
320      POKE 5185,N
330      SYS 5120
340      DATA 10,13,5,10,13,5,10,13,10
350      DATA 10,13,5,162,14,5,162,14,10
360      DATA 247,10,10,10,13,5,10,13,5
370      DATA 103,17,5,137,19,13,237,21,5
380      DATA 237,21,10,237,21,5,237,21,10
390      DATA 137,19,10,137,19,10,103,17,10
400      DATA 103,17,20,237,21,5,237,21,13
410      DATA 59,23,10,237,21,5,237,21,5
420      DATA 237,21,13,137,19,30,237,21,8
430      DATA 137,19,8,137,19,15,103,17,15
440      DATA 103,17,30,103,17,13,10,13,5
450      DATA 10,13,5,10,13,10,162,14,10
460      DATA 103,17,5,10,13,5,10,13,10
470      DATA 10,13,10,103,17,5,137,19,13
480      DATA 137,19,5,237,21,13,237,21,10
490      DATA 137,19,5,137,19,5,137,19,5
500      DATA 103,17,10,103,17,5,103,17,20
510      DATA 237,21,5,237,21,13,59,23,10
520      DATA 237,21,5,237,21,5,237,21,13
530      DATA 137,19,30,237,21,10,137,19,10
540      DATA 137,19,10,103,17,15,103,17,30
550      DATA 237,21,5,137,19,10,103,17,5
560      DATA 103,17,20,237,21,5,20,26,10
570      DATA 69,29,5,69,29,10,20,26,10
580      DATA 20,26,5,20,26,10,237,21,5
590      DATA 237,21,5,137,19,5,103,17,10
600      DATA 162,14,5,10,13,10,237,21,5
610      DATA 237,21,10,103,17,30,237,21,5
620      DATA 237,21,10,59,23,5,59,23,10
630      DATA 237,21,5,237,21,5,237,21,10
```

```
640    DATA 137,19,30,237,21,10,137,19,10
650    DATA 137,19,10,137,19,13,103,17,13
660    DATA 103,17,30,247,10,5,10,13,5
```

This tune may bore you after a while, so we'll now give you some ground rules for putting in your own tunes. A song can have up to 255 notes, with every note entered in this format:

Frequency	(low-byte)
Frequency	(high-byte)
Duration	(how long it is to be held)

You can choose your own notes. For example, we called up a frequency of 3338 (in low/high format, 10 and 13) for a G. Our duration was 10 (like an average quarter note). Line 230 will have to be changed to adjust for your song length. When you want to change waveforms, put POKE 7226,WF (waveform) at the end of the program. WF has the following functions:

17	TRIANGLE WAVE
33	SAWTOOTH WAVE
65	PULSE WAVE
129	NOISE

This program operates voice three ONLY. You could convert the program to include the first and second voices of the SID chip. If you want to program this routine in machine language, we've included that listing below. This routine works with the IRQ vectors:

$1400 (5120)   Routine which moves IRQ vectors to $1415 (5141)

$1416 (5142)   Start of music/IRQ routine till $144E (5198)

$14F1 (5361)   Count duration; when 1CF1=0, go to next note

$14F3 (5363)   Note counter

$1500 (5376)   Memory for low-byte of note to $15FF (5631)

$1600 (5632)   Memory for high-byte of note to $16FF (5887)

$1700 (5888)   Memory for all note values to $17FF (6143)

Once you have a look at the commented listing, you'll have a good idea of the program's inner workings. You can use our BASIC loader, or type this in on your monitor:

```
1400 78         SEI             ;Hinder interrupt
1401 A9 16      LDA #$16        ;Set IRQ vector to
1403 8D 14 03   STA $0314       ;start of the
1406 A9 14      LDA #$14        ;music routine
1408 8D 15 03   STA $0315
140B 58         CLI             ;Enable interrupt
140C A0 00      LDY #$00
140E 8C F3 14   STY $14F3
1411 C8         INY
1412 8C F1 14   STY $14F1
1415 60         RTS             ;Return to BASIC
1416 CE F1 14   DEC 14F1        ;Decrement counter
1419 D0 31      BNE 144C        ;Counter >0, then
                                 continue count
141B 48         PHA             ;Accu on stack
141C 8D 00 FF   STA $FF00       ;switches I/O
141F 8D 12 D4   STA $D412       ;Waveform = 0
1422 8A         TXA             ;X-reg into accumulator
1423 48         PHA             ;Accu to stack
1424 AE F3 14   LDX $14F3       ;Number for new note
1427 BD 00 16   LDA $1500,X     ;Get note low byte
142A 8D 0E D4   STA $D40E       ;Set low byte
142D BD 00 16   LDA $1600,X     ;Get high byte
1430 8D 0F D4   STA $D40F       ;Set high byte
1433 BD 00 17   LDA $1700,X     ;Get note value
```

```
1436 8D F1 14  STA $14F1      ;Set counter
1439 A9 41      LDA #$41       ;Load waveform
143B 8D 12 D4  STA $D412      ;Set waveform
143E E8         INX            ;Raise note counter
143F 38         SEC
1440 E0 63      CPX #$63       ;Last note?
1442 90 02      BCC $1446      ;NO--then $1C46
1444 A2 00      LDX #$00       ;Note counter at 0
1446 8E F3 14  STX $14F3      ;Store note counter
1449 68         PLA            ;Accu from stack
144A AA         TAX            ;X-reg = accu
144B 68         PLA            ;Accu from stack
144C 4C 65 FA  JMP $FA65      ;Goto normal IRQ
```

3.5 REAL-TIME CLOCK ON THE C-128

These days, time is important to all of us. Perhaps this is on reason why
most computers now have built-in clocks. By making use of the built-in
variable TI$, your C-128 can become a clock. Be forewarned that TI$ runs
unevenly at times; because of this we have developed a real-time clock using
CIA #1:

```
20      REM  0
30      DATA 31,248,,63,252,
40      DATA 127,254,,255,255,,240,15,
50      DATA 224,7,,224,7,,224,7,,224,7,
60      DATA 224,7,,224,7,,224,7,,224,7,
70      DATA 224,7,,224,7,,224,7,,224,7,
80      DATA 240,15,,255,255,,127,254,
90      DATA 63,252,,
100     REM  1
110     DATA 3,252,,7,254,,7,254,
120     DATA 7,254,,7,254,,3,254,
130     DATA ,126,,,126,,,126,,,126,,,126,
140     DATA ,126,,,126,,,126,,,126,,,126,
150     DATA ,126,,,126,,,126,,,126,,,60,,
```

```
160     REM    2
170     DATA   63,254,,127,255,,127,255,
180     DATA   124,31,,120,15,,48,15,,,15,
190     DATA   ,31,,,63,,,126,,,252,,1,248,
200     DATA   3,240,,7,224,,15,192,,31,134,
210     DATA   63,7,,126,7,,252,7,,255,255,
220     DATA   127,254,,
230     REM    3
240     DATA   63,254,,127,255,,127,255,
250     DATA   124,31,,120,15,,48,15,,,31,
260     DATA   ,63,,,127,,,255,,1,255,
270     DATA   1,255,,,255,
280     DATA   ,127,,,63,,96,31,,240,15,
290     DATA   240,15,,255,255,
300     DATA   255,255,,127,254,,
310     REM    4
320     DATA   ,124,,,252,,1,252,,1,252,
330     DATA   3,252,,3,252,,7,252,,7,252,
340     DATA   15,188,,15,188,,31,60,,31,60,
350     DATA   62,60,,124,60,,248,60,
360     DATA   255,255,,255,255,,255,255,
370     DATA   255,255,,,60,,,60,,
380     REM    5
390     DATA   127,252,,255,255,,255,255,
400     DATA   240,15,,224,15,,224,6,,240,,
410     DATA   255,,,255,224,,127,248,
420     DATA   1,254,,,127,,,31,,,31,,,31,
430     DATA   ,31,,96,127,,241,254,,255,248,
440     DATA   255,224,,127,128,,
450     REM    6
460     DATA   127,252,,255,255,,255,255,
470     DATA   240,15,,224,15,,224,6,,240,,
480     DATA   255,,,255,224,,255,248,,248
490     DATA   254,,240,127,,224,31,,224,31,,224,31,
500     DATA   224,31,,240,127,,248,254,,255,248,
510     DATA   255,224,,127,128,,
520     REM    7
530     DATA   63,254,,127,255,,127,255,
540     DATA   124,31,,120,15,,48,15,,,15,
550     DATA   ,31,,,63,,,126,,,252,,1,248,
560     DATA   3,240,,7,224,,15,192,,31,128,
570     DATA   63,,,126,,,252,,,252,,,252,,,
580     REM    8
```

```
590     DATA 127,254,,255,255,,255,255,
600     DATA 240,15,,224,7,,240,15,
610     DATA 255,255,,255,255,,127,254,
620     DATA 127,254,,254,127,,240,15,
630     DATA 224,7,,224,7,,224,7,,224,7,
640     DATA 240,15,,127,254,,31,248,
650     DATA 15,224,,1,128,,
660     REM   9
670     DATA 1,254,,7,255,,31,255,,127,143,
680     DATA 254,15,,240,15,,240,15,
690     DATA 240,15,,240,15,,254,15,
700     DATA 127,143,,31,254,,7,255,,1,255,
710     DATA ,15,,96,7,,240,7,,240,15,
720     DATA 255,255,,255,255,,127,254,,
730     REM: POKE 56334, PEEK (56334) OR 128
740     FOR I = 3456 TO 4095
750     READ A
760     POKE I,A
770     NEXT I
780     REM   SET TIME
790     INPUT "HOURS{SPACE}{SPACE}{SPACE}";S
800     IF S > 12 THEN S = S - 12:   GOTO 800
810     IF S < 0 THEN 790
820     POKE 56331,S +  INT (S / 10) * 6
830     INPUT "MINUTES{SPACE}";M
840     IF M < 0 OR M > 59 THEN 830
850     POKE 56330,M +  INT (M / 10) * 6
860     INPUT "SECONDS{SPACE}";S
870     IF S < 0 OR S > 59 THEN 860
880     POKE 56329,S +  INT (S / 10) * 6
890     S = 0
900     FOR I = 5120 TO 5180
910     READ A
920     S = S + A
930     POKE I,A
940     NEXT I
950     IF S <> 6300 THEN PRINT "?ERROR IN DATA":END
960     PRINT "{CLR HOME}HIT RETURN TO START"
965     GET A$:   IF A$ <  >  CHR$ (13) THEN 965
970     POKE 56328,0
980     SYS 5120
990     DATA 120,169,13,141,20,3,169
1000    DATA 20,141,21,3,88,96,160
```

```
1010    DATA 3,173,11,220,41,31,76
1020    DATA 26,20,185,8,220,41,240
1030    DATA 74,74,74,74
1040    DATA 72,185,8,220,41,15
1050    DATA 72,136,208,237,173,8
1060    DATA 220,72,160,7,104
1070    DATA 24,105,54,153,247,7,136
1080    DATA 208,246,76,101,250
1090    FOR I = 1 TO 7
1100    SPRITE I,1,1,1,0,1,0
1110    MOVSPR I,30 + I * 20 + INT((I-1)/2) * 10,100
1120    NEXT I
```

The individual numbers are actually sprites. In fact, most of the listing is
just to define the sprites. If you prefer, you can run the program without
sprites; just type in the program beginning at line 780 and ending at line
1080. You will need to alter the checksum (to "6298"), and change line
1070 to:

```
1070 DATA 24,105,48,153,255,3,136
```

Now for the machine language listing:

```
1400  78           SEI               ;Interrupt off
1401  A9 0D        LDA #$00          ;Set IRQ vector
1403  8D 14 03     STA $0314         ;to beginning of
1406  A9 14        LDA #$14          ;this routine
1408  8D 15 03     STA $0315
140B  58           CLI               ;Enable interrupt
140C  60           RTS               ;Return to BASIC
140D  A0 03        LDY #$03
140F  AD 0C DC     LDA $DC0B         ;Hour setting
1412  29 1F        AND #$1F          ;only first 5 bits
1414  4C 1A 14     JMP $141A
1417  B9 08 DC     LDA $DC08,Y;Time
141A  29 F0        AND #$F0          ;only decimal point
141C  4A           LSR               ;Shift bit 4-7
141D  4A           LSR               ;to bits 0-3
```

```
141E 4A          LSR
141F 4A          LSR
1420 48          PHA           ;Put number on stack
1421 B9 08 DC    LDA $DC08,Y;Time
1424 29 0F       AND #$0F      ;Seconds
1426 48          PHA           ;Put time on stack
1427 88          DEY
1428 D0 ED       BNE $1417
142A AD 08 DC    LDA $DC08     ;Tenths
142D 48          PHA           ;Put tenths on stack
142E A0 07       LDY #$07
1430 68          PLA           ;Get count from stack
1431 18          CLC
1432 69 36       ADC #$36      ;Add start-of-sprites
1434 99 F7 07    STA $07F7,Y;Sprite on block
1437 88          DEY
1438 D0 F6       BNE 1430
143A 4C 65 FA    JMP $FA65     ;Goto normal IRQ
```

The "other" version (without sprites) requires changing only two lines:

```
1432 69 30       ADC #$30      ;Convert count into ASCII
1434 99 FF 03 STA $03FF,Y;and put onscreen
```

As you can see from the listing, you could set the clock using the IRQ. The clock will shut down when <RUN STOP/RESTORE> is pressed.

3.6 ANALOG CLOCK

To emphasize the importance of time, here's another clock program. Since not everyone likes digital clocks, this is an analog clock, from which most of us learned to tell time in the first place. This program combines a time program and the C-128's graphic commands. This program only works on a 40-column screen.

Now on to the program. It's divided into two parts. The first part should look familiar to you, since it was used for setting the clock in the previous chapter. The second section of the program begins at line 150. This is where the clock face and hands are drawn, and where the second hand is controlled. Every minute, the screen is redrawn. The hands are all drawn using an extension of the CIRCLE command.

```
10       REM  SET CLOCK
20       INPUT "HOURS{SPACE 3}";S
30       IF S > 12 THEN S = S - 12:  GOTO 30
40       IF S < 0 THEN 20
50       POKE 56331,S +  INT (S / 10) * 6
60       INPUT "MINUTES{SPACE}";M
70       IF M < 0 OR M > 59 THEN 60
80       POKE 56330,M +  INT (M / 10) * 6
90       INPUT "SECONDS{SPACE}";S
100      IF S < 0 OR S > 59 THEN 90
110      POKE 56329,S +  INT (S / 10) * 6
120      PRINT "HIT RETURN TO START CLOCK"
125      GET A$:  IF A$ <>  CHR$ (13) THEN 125
130      REM: POKE 56334, PEEK (56334) OR 128
140      POKE 56328,0
150      REM  DRAW CLOCK
160      GRAPHIC 1
170      SCNCLR
180      COLOR 1,2
```

```
200     CIRCLE ,160,100,74
210     CHAR ,19,4,"12"
220     CHAR ,20,21,"6"
230     CHAR ,28,12,"3"
240     CHAR ,11,12,"9"
270     REM   DRAW HOUR AND MINUTE HAND
280     COLOR 1,12
290     M =INT(PEEK(56330)/16)*10+(PEEK(56330)AND15)
300     COLOR 1,1
310     CIRCLE ,160,100,0,60,40,90,M * 6
320     H = ((16 AND  PEEK(56331))/16)*10 +
        (PEEK (56331) AND 15)
330     CIRCLE ,160,100,0,60,60,90,H * 30 + M / 2
340     REM   DRAW SECOND HAND
350     WAIT 56328,8
360     COLOR 1,12
370     CIRCLE ,160,100,0,110,0,40,S * 6
380     COLOR 1,2
390     S=INT(PEEK(56329)/16)*10 +(PEEK(56329)AND15)
400     CIRCLE ,160,100,0,110,0,40,S * 6
410     IF S = 0 THEN 170
420     GOTO 350
```

3.7 LLIST

There are times when you'd like a quick printout of a BASIC program.
Commodore BASIC doesn't make a hardcopy listing easy. You must enter
all of the following commands:

```
OPEN4,4:CMD 4:LIST:CLOSE4
```

Other versions of BASIC have the command LLIST. The C-128 has to
enable printer output only, jump to LIST, and turn back to the screen.

The following LLIST routine will not go directly to the LIST command at the beginning, but a little later. It won't check for which lines to list (you'd want the entire program in hardcopy anyway). Vectors $61/$62 come into play here (pointing to the beginning of the first line to be listed). Here's the assembler listing:

```
1A00 A9 OO      LDA  #$00      :Configuration
1A02 8D 00 FF   STA $FF00      :Set configuration
1A05 A9 OO      LDA #$00       :File name
1A07 20 BD FF   JSR $FFBD      :Set file name
1A0A A9 04      LDA #$04       :Logical file number
1A0C AA         TAX            :Device number
1A0D A0 00      LDY #$07       :Secondary address
1A0F 20 BA FF   JSR $FFBA      :Set file parameters
1A12 20 C0 FF   JSR $FFC0      :Kernal routine OPEN
1A15 A2 04      LDX #$04       :Logical file number
1A17 20 C9 FF   JSR $FFC9      :Set output device
1A1A A5 2D      LDA $2D        :BASIC RAM start--low
1A1C 85 61      STA $61        :store
1A1E A5 2E      LDA $2E        :BASIC RAM start--high
1A20 85 62      STA $62        :store
1A22 20 E5 50   JSR $50E5      :LIST routine (list all)
1A25 A9 OO      LDA  #$00      :Configuration
1A27 8D 00 FF   STA $FF00      :Set configuration
1A2A A9 04      LDA #$04       :Logical file number
1A2C 20 C3 FF   JSR $FFE7      :Kernal routine CLALL
1A2F 60         RTS            :Return
```

Run this routine by entering SYS DEC("1A00") and your program will be listed to the printer.

Here is the BASIC loader:

```
100 FOR X = 6656 TO 6703
110 READ A : CS = CS + A: POKE X, A
120 NEXT X
130 DATA 169,0,141,0,255,169,0,32,189,255
```

```
140 DATA 169,4,170,160,7,32,186,255,32,192
150 DATA 255,162,4,32,201,255,165,45,133,97
160 DATA 165,46,133,98,32,228,80,169,0,141
170 DATA 0,255,169,4,32,231,255,96
```

3.8 DO-IT-YOURSELF WORD PROCESSING

Writing about full-fledged word processing doesn't make a lot of sense in a "Tricks and Tips" book. Instead, we'll offer you a quick idea that will do for throwing a quick memo on paper—in effect, a cheap imitation of a word processing program.

First, type in AUTO 10 <RETURN>. Now type in your first line number (10), followed by a line of text and <RETURN> (you'll have to do this at the end of every line, but it's a small price to pay). Watch your line length (60 characters [1 1/2 lines] will work), since the printer will receive this verbatim. Here's a sample of text:

```
10 This is the new word processor which
20 is using built-in commands.  The quick
30 brown fox jumped over the lazy warthog.
40 ...
```

Great, but how do we get it on paper? Simple; type in this line in direct mode when you're through entering text:

```
POKE 24,37:OPEN4,4:CMD 4:LIST:PRINT#4:CLOSE4
```

The text prints out—without the line numbers!

You can SAVE this text to diskette or cassette as you would a normal program, and print it out later. Who knows? Maybe sooner or later you'll end up developing your own professional word processing software.

Address 24 can do an amazing number of things. For example:

```
POKE 24,37:LIST
```

lists a program on the screen without line numbers. If you run into a "FORMULA TOO COMPLEX ERROR", just try

```
POKE 24,27
```

Values other than 27 used in address 24 can make some changes to BASIC listings. Be careful. Error messages will reset the contents of location 24.

3.9 MODIFIED INPUT

BASIC 7.0 has all those input commands you "grew up with" on the C-64; GET and INPUT, and a new one: GETKEY.

INPUT, however, isn't especially aesthetic—you get a question mark at every prompt onscreen. Sometimes a question mark isn't appropriate, as in

```
10 INPUT"INPUT YOUR NAME!";N$
```

One method of getting around this is to open your screen as a file. Try this out instead of the normal INPUT statement:

```
10 OPEN 1,0 :REM (screen as a file)
20 INPUT#1,A$: REM (input w/o ?)
30 CLOSE 1
```

Now, if the INPUT command has to be in a particular spot on the screen, add the following:

```
20 CHAR,column, row
25 PRINT" ";:
27 INPUT#1,A$
```

CHAR positions the cursor much like a PRINT AT statement.

3.10 WARNING TONE

When the first typewriters appeared, they had a warning bell to let you know that you were getting close to the right margin. This can still be useful on computers. Here's a machine language program to create such a function:

```
142D A9 FF       LDA #$FF        ;Musical values
142F 8D 06 D4    STA $D406
1432 8D 18 D4    STA $D418
1435 A9 09       LDA #$09
1437 8D 05 D4    STA $D405
143A 78          SEI             ;Interrupt off
143B A9 47       LDA #$47        ;Reset IRQ vector
143D 8D 14 03    STA $0314
1440 A0 14       LDA #$14
```

```
1442 8D 15 03   STA $0315
1445 58         CLI              ;Enable IRQ
1446 60         RTS              ;Return to BASIC
1447 48         PHA              ;Accu on stack
1448 A5 E7      LDA $E7          ;Load right margin
144A E5 EC      SBC $EC          ;Draw cursor-column
144C C9 02      CMP #$02         ;=2?
144E D0 11      BNE $1461        ;NO--then $1461
1450 CD 80 14   CMP $1480        ;Column by last
1453 F0 0F      BEQ $1464        ;IRQ also 2, then $1464
1455 8D 80 14   STA $1480        ;Store 2
1458 A9 A0      LDA #$A0         ;Play tone
145A 8D 01 D4   STA $D401
145D A9 21      LDA #$21
145F D0 05      BNE $1466
1461 8D 80 14   STA $1480        ;Store column
1464 A9 00      LDA #$00         ;Turn tone off
1466 8D 01 D4   STA $D401
1469 8D 00 D4   STA $D400
146C 8D 04 D4   STA $D404        ;Set waveform
146F 68         PLA              ;Accu from stack
1470 4C 65 FA   JMP $FA65        ;Jump to IRQ
1480 Pointer for previous column.
```

Two characters from the end-of-line, a tone will sound. This is standard; it
doesn't change if you switch from TV to a monitor. Basically, the program
counts from the right margin of a window -- this is where the current cursor
position is drawn.

```
10      REM   WARNING TONE
20      FOR I = 5165 TO 5234
30      READ A
40      S = S + A
50      POKE I,A
60      NEXT I
70      IF S < > 8167 THEN BEGIN
80      PRINT "?ERROR{SPACE}IN{SPACE}DATA"
90      END
100     BEND
110     SYS 5165
```

```
120     DATA 169,255,141,6,212,141,24,212
130     DATA 169,9,141,5,212,120,169,71
140     DATA 141,20,3,169,20,141,21,3,88,96
150     DATA 72,165,231,229,236,201,2,208
160     DATA 17,205,128,20,240,15,141,128
170     DATA 20,169,160,141,1,212,169,33
180     DATA 208,5,141,128,20,169,0,141
190     DATA 1,212,141,0,212,141,4,212
200     DATA 104,76,101,250
```

You can change the value to anything *except* the last column. Just bear in mind that this routine is counting from right to left:

```
POKE 5197,N
```

N will give you your new "warning" location.

This routine would be great for word processing, or for other data input especially when used in combination with the "Keyboard Beep" program in Chapter 7.

CHAPTER 4

SOFTWARE PROTECTION ON THE C-128

Software publishers invest a lot of time and money in copy protection. It's really pretty sad that software piracy is running rampant. Pirates are taking money out of the author's hand. The author is writing software to make a profit, but if the pirate is stealing software, then this is a disincentive to the author to produce more quality software.

You can install copy protection on your own disks. The protection isn't unbreakable, but it will make matters difficult for the curious. One form of protection is based on a staple of BASIC programming: the LIST command. We'll talk about other methods of getting in the "back door" of protection.

4.1 PROTECTION WITH COLONS

We did a lot of research and experimentation into protection routines. We found a few small BASIC routines for you to try. For example, you can hide individual lines from nosy folks with five colons! Type this:

```
450 :::::PRINT "(C) 1985 by 'The Team'"
```

Next, add this routine to your programs with five colons inserted in the lines you wish to hide:

```
60000    LI = 45
60005    BA = LI
60010    LI = PEEK (LI) + 256 * PEEK (LI+1)
60020    IF LI = 0 THEN PRINT "DONE!" : END
60030    PRINT CHR$(145); "PASS ";
         PEEK(BA+2)+256*PEEK(BA+3);
60040    PRINT X$
60050    BA = LI
60060    FOR X = 4 TO 8
60070    IF PEEK (LI+X) <> ASC(:) THEN X=8: FL=1
60080    NEXT X
60090    IF FL = 1 THEN FL = 0 : GOTO 60010
60100    POKE LI + 4, 0 : X$ = X$ + "*"
60110    GOTO 60010
```

The routine is activated with RUN 60000. It tests for program lines to be
ignored (PASS). When it finds one, the line will be covered with asterisks.
The system will say READY when it's done; all that remains is for you to
DELETE 60000- . Run the program; works fine. Now LIST it; the line
numbers of the protected lines appear, but the contents of the lines are
invisible.

The Program:

60000:   Start-of-BASIC is stored in variable LI. If you want to use this
          program in C-64 mode, you'll have to change the parameters in
          locations 45 and 43.

60010 :   Rather than look at *every* byte in the program, the protection
          routine checks line links for colons; the routine runs faster that
          way.

60020 :   Program ends when line link LI=0.

60030 :   Current line number given.

60040 :   Number of protected lines is stored in X$.

60050 :   Basis of new line starting range is equal to the contents of link LI.

60060 :   Routine looks at first five characters of a line.

60080 :   Each "normal" line sets flag FL, and X to 8.

60090 :   If FL=1 the flag is reset, and the next line observed.

60100 :   Line is protected; first colon is set to 0. When the program sees the 0, it's interpreted as an end-of-line, and the line is treated as if it were non-existent.

4.2 LINE NUMBER ROULETTE

A prime characteristic of BASIC is its sequential line numbers, which act as a guide for the programmer. Line numbers larger than 64000 cannot be used. We can use this little fact to our advantage: Type in this routine.

```
60000   BA = PEEK (45) + 256 * PEEK (46)
60010   LI = PEEK (BA) + 256 * PEEK (BA + 1)
60020   IF LI = 0 THEN PRINT "DONE!"  : END
60030   PRINT"FIND LINE:"; PEEK(BA+2)+256*PEEK(BA+3)
60040   PRINT "(C)HANGE   (G)O ON   (E)ND  ?"
60050   GETKEY A$
```

```
60060    IF A$ = "E" THEN PRINT "OK" : END
60070    IF A$ = "G" THEN 60140
60080    INPUT "NEW LINE NUMBER"; ZN$
60090    IF ZN < 0 OR ZN > 65535 THEN 60080
60100    HI = INT(ZN/256) : LO= ZN-(256*HI)
60110    POKE BA+2, LO
60120    POKE BA+3, HI
60130    PRINT CHR$(145);
60140    BA = LI
60150    PRINT CHR$(145);CHR$(145);
60160    GOTO 60010
```

The first line probably looks familiar to you. Start the routine; the system will go through each line with prompts. You have three options: (C) HANGE, (G) O ON, or (E) ND. C alters the program line; G looks for the next line; and E ends the program. There are a few limitations:

a)   GOTO and GOSUB line numbers are unaltered.

b)   Line numbers larger than 64000 cannot be deleted.

c)   All line numbers less than one cannot be jumped to.

The Program:

The principle of this routine is pretty simple: It looks at all the BASIC program lines. If the line number is changed, the new line number is stored in ZN and in line 60100 in low/high-byte format. Then, the new value is POKEd over the old in BASIC memory.

This protection will be automatically saved on disk or cassette with the program itself.

One other thing: type in a line, say, 64000. Now run the routine, and change it to 65535. This produces two effects. First, a line with the number 65535 is essentially considered to be the end of the program. Second, that high number is not shown if it's a REM, so you could hide your copyright notice there.

4.3 MANIPULATING LINE-LINKS

The preceding routine worked on the so-called line-links to change line numbers. Let's take another shot at "bending" these line-links, specifically, adjusting the link pointing to the next line. When we do this, the next line is invisible. Or, if you wish, we could fix a line-link to list the same line over and over. Usually, this won't bother the program run, unless you've really gone wild with these adjustments. Type this in by hand:

```
60000 INPUT "1. LINE NUMBER"; Z1
60020 INPUT "2. LINE NUMBER"; Z2
60020 BA = 45
60030 BA = PEEK (BA) + 256*PEEK(BA+1)
60040 IF BA=0 THEN PRINT "LINE DOES NOT EXIST!":END
60050 ZN = PEEK(BA+2) +256*PEEK(BA+3)
60060 IF FL = 0 THEN IF ZN =Z1 THEN
      L1=BA:L2=BA+1:FL=1
60070 IF FL = 0 THEN 60030
60080 IF ZN=22 THEN POKE L1,PEEK(BA)  :
      POKE L2,PEEK(BA+1):END
60090 GOTO 60030
```

The routine will ask you for the numbers of the first and second program lines. The links in the first line pointing to both lines will be altered. All lines become invisible. One thing to remember with this routine: any alterations (adding or deleting lines) recalculate the line-link pointers, so it's a far from infallible protection trick.

4.4   CREATIVE CONTROL CHARACTERS: MAKING GREMLINS

Control characters are a familiar sight; for example, this one clears the screen: "♥". We see them in quote mode, they change character position and color. There is another use for these characters, though: we can use them on the screen to foil LISTing. Type this in first in direct mode:

```
KEY1,CHR$(27)+CHR$(79)+"{RVSON}{SHIFT-M}{RVSOFF}"+
CHR$(34)+CHR$(20)
```

This turns <F1> into an instant <SHIFT-M> (this activates control characters). Let's have some fun with a few BASIC lines (whenever an asterisk (*) appears, press <F1>).

The Gremlin and PRINT

```
 PRINT"This is how it works*in PRINT statements*!"
```

All <SHIFT-M> does here is perform a carriage return (C/R). This has nothing to do with software protection; just showing you what it does.

The Gremlin and REM

```
10 REM"*(CRSRUP)(RVSON)This is a test line
```

List this line, things are getting interesting now! The <SHIFT-M> causes the two control characters to execute, so the line moves up one line and goes into reverse video. In other words, the REM acts like a PRINT statement when listed!

The possibilities are almost limitless! We can change colors...

```
1000 REM"*(CTRL+1to8)
1000 REM"*(C= + 1to8)
```

...format listings...

```
1000 REM"*(CRSRDOWN)(CRSRDOWN)
```

...or simply mask lines out:

```
1000 REM"*{CRSRUP}900 SYS (4096) CRACKED BY RUSS T
```
(Indicates cracked machine language program)

```
1000 PRINT"(C) BY RUSS T":REM"*{CRSRUP}
```
(Line 1000 overwritten by next line)

Have a good time!

4.5 PROTECTION WITH POKES

POKEs can do so much; they even give you the ability to ward off saving, listing or running a program. One disadvantage: The program has to be RUN before any of this will take effect, but you can sidestep this somewhat by using an autoboot program.

4.5.1 LIST DISABLING

Page 3 has a pointer that points to the vector for the LIST input. This vector has the addresses 774/775 ($0306/$0307). Try POKE 774,61:POKE 775,255. Now LIST. The computer acts as if you've requested a warm-start, and goes to the opening screen. Now try POKE 774,38:POKE 775,160, which points to the vector for "RTS". Only line numbers will be given.

As you can see, changing pointers can do remarkable things.

4.5.2 DISABLING RUN-STOP/RESTORE

Early in computing, people got the idea of putting code words into programs. Commodore computers can be circumvented, just by pressing <RUN-STOP/RESTORE>, and looking up the code word in the program. We can foil that with POKE 808,PEEK(808)-3 which disables both keys.

Let's put it into practice:

```
10 POKE 808,PEEK(808)-3
20 PRINT"This is a test ";
30 GET A$:IF A$=CHR$(3) THEN PRINT:PRINT"BREAK"
```

POKE 792,51:POKE 793,255 disables RESTORE alone; <RUN-STOP>
alone can be done in BASIC:

```
10 TRAP 1000
20 PRINT"This is a test ";
30 GOTO 20
1000 ?"*BREAK*"
1010 RESUME NEXT
```

Here we used the message "BREAK" to signify the <RUN-STOP> key.
See the chapter on "Error Handling" (Chap. 3). One final word: This
routine can be skirted by pressing the <RUN-STOP> key quickly several
times.

4.5.3 DISABLING SAVE

The SAVE vector also resides in page 3 of memory (818/819
[$0332/$0333]). We can pretty much pull the same stuff that we did in the
LIST disable: RTS, reset, etc.

4.6 DISK COPY PROTECTION

So far, we've looked at general in-program protection. Next, we're going to look at what's involved in protecting a disk from copying.

Perhaps you've heard of "destroying" the tracks on a disk. We can create a READ ERROR, which will at least slow down disk copying. Name the track you wish to change in the variable TR.

```
 0 REM READ ERROR ON DISK
10 OPEN 1,8,15
20 OPEN 2,8,2,"#"
30 PRINT#1,"U1 2 0";TR;0
40 PRINT#1,"M-E"CHR$(163)CHR$(253)
```

Before starting, make sure there's no valuable disk in the drive.

4.7 LOAD "$"

There are times when you may want to try stopping anyone from reading the disk directory, since the directory gives important information to the would-be copier. Best way around this is to wipe the directory altogether!

```
10  REM DIRECTORY SCRATCH
20  OPEN 1,8,3,"#"
30  OPEN 2,8,15,"B-P3,144"
40  PRINT#1,CHR$(20)CHR$(20)CHR$(20)CHR$(0)CHR$(0)
    CHR$(0)
50  PRINT#2,"U2:3,0,18"
60  PRINT#2,"I"
70  END
```

Use this program with disks from which you've memorized the program names. Also, keep in mind that you won't know what programs have been changed, scratched, or whatever.

Essentially, when the directory is loaded with LOAD "$",8 it is handled like a BASIC program. We simply write a zero to the beginning of the directory, and the LIST routine interprets the zero as the end-of-program. This only works for LOAD"$",8 and not the DIRECTORY command.

CHAPTER 5

SELF-MODIFYING PROGRAMS

5.1 LINE INSERTION

Programs are usually designed with just one application in mind, partially due to the fact that you can't change programs as they're running. In the next few pages, we're going to show you how to insert lines into a running program. We'll also give you some sample applications for this useful feature.

Inserting lines in an running program opens up a new spectrum of programming, and can be accomplished with a few simple POKEs. Remember, though, this little routine is a big step from a program generator, which lets you create a BASIC (or other) program.

Technically, this line addition is very complicated. So, the normal procedure is to stop the program, insert the line and restart the program. The key to our work in this chapter is the keyboard buffer. Try this test program:

```
10  TP=842
20  POKE    TP,ASC("L")
30  POKE  TP+1,ASC("I")
40  POKE  TP+2,ASC("S")
50  POKE  TP+3,ASC("T")
60  POKE  TP+4,13: REM RETURN
70:
80  POKE 208,5
90  END
```

RUNning this program makes it LIST itself by writing LIST into the keyboard buffer (lines 20-50) and <RETURN> (line 60). Line 80 tells the operating system that five characters are in the keyboard buffer. One application would be for INPUT or GET, or for a program end. This is what happens: the program ends at line 90, but the computer "INPUTS" the characters that were "stuck" in the keyboard buffer. So, the system interprets LIST<RETURN> as a direct command. Remember that the computer gets the characters when the program ends. Experiment -- put in your own commands (e.g., RUN; but remember to put in <RETURN>s (13)).

5.2 FORMULA ENTRY

Now, let's experiment with changing lines in a running BASIC program:

```
10 PRINT"FORMULA ENTRY"
20 PRINT:PRINT
30 PRINT"ENTER AN EQUATION"
40 PRINT"(E.G. Y=2*X+SQR(X/34.5)*INT(5.6*X^4)
50 INPUT V$
```

This program section needs no detailed explanation. Basically, the equation of your choice is typed in, and stored in V$. Our example has the format Y=....X... , which leaves X open for any variable. But how do we get the equation into the program?

```
60 PRINT CHR$(147)
70 PRINT : PRINT"1000";V$
80 PRINT : PRINT"RUN 500"
```

This creates a new line number -- line 1000 with your formula.

```
90 PRINT CHR$(19);
```

When you RUN this program, the cursor blinks on the new line. If the line is correct, press the <RETURN> key. Here's more:

```
100  FOR A=0 TO 3
110  POKE 842+A,13
120  NEXT A
130  POKE 208,4
140  END
500  PRINT CHR$(147)
510  INPUT "X-VALUE";X
1000 REM HERE'S WHERE THE EQUATION GOES
1010 PRINT"RESULT IS:";Y
1020 END
```

The keyboard buffer is filled with the ASCII code for <RETURN>. The program ends, the <RETURN>s are sent, and the routine automatically starts with RUN 500. Be sure you make the proper changes when a larger number of variables are used; this is a matter of altering line 500.

5.3 DATA STATEMENT GENERATOR

We're not through with this subject and the next program will show that. This is a "real" application program: a DATA generator, which you'll find to be useful. Although this program lends itself to alterations, it generates a lot of lines!

```
10      PRINT "{CLR HOME}D A T A - G E N E R A T O R"
20      PRINT :  PRINT :  PRINT
30      PRINT "THIS PROGRAM CONVERTS THE ";
40      IF  PEEK (215) < 128 THEN  PRINT
50      PRINT "CONTENTS OF MEMORY TO A BASIC-LOADER!"
60      PRINT :  PRINT
70      PRINT "I N P U T - F O R M A T :  "
80      PRINT :  PRINT
90      INPUT "MEMORY CONFIGURATION (BANK)";BK
100      INPUT "BEGINNING DATA ADDRESS (HEX)";A$
110      INPUT "ENDING DATA ADDRESS (HEX)";B$
120      A =  DEC (A$) - 1: B =  DEC (B$)
130      :
140      INPUT "BEGINNING LINE NUMBER";Z: O = Z
150      INPUT "LINE NUMBER INCREMENT";S
160      INPUT "AMOUNT OF DATA PER LINE";DZ: XY = DZ
170      :
180      GOSUB 1000
190      :
200      LD = B - A
210      PRINT "{CLR HOME}{CRSR DOWN}{CRSR DOWN}"
220      IF LD < DZ THEN DZ = LD: FL = 1
230      LD = LD - DZ
240      PRINT Z;"DATA ";
250      IF DZ > 1 THEN  FOR W = 1 TO DZ - 1:
         ELSE  GOTO 290
260      BANK BK: P =  PEEK (A + W + (XY * ZE)):
         PRINT P;"{CRSR LEFT},";
270      CS = CS + P
280      NEXT W
290      ZE = ZE + 1
300      BANK BK: P =  PEEK (A + (XY * (ZE-1)) + DZ):
         PRINT P: CS = CS + P
310      :
320      Z = Z + S
330      IF FL = 0 THEN  PRINT "GOTO 210":
         ELSE  PRINT "GOTO 900"
340      GOTO 800
800      REM  FILL KEYBOARD BUFFER
810      PRINT "{HOME}";
820      FOR X = 842 TO 851
830      POKE X,13
840      NEXT X
```

```
850      POKE   DEC ("D0"),10
860      END
900      REM   EDITOR
910      PRINT "{CLR HOME}{CRSR DOWN}{CRSR DOWN}";
920      PRINT O+3*S;"IF CS<>";CS;
         " THEN PRINT CHR$(7);: LIST"
930      PRINT "DELETE -1300"
940      BANK 15:  GOTO 800
1000     REM   INIT
1010     PRINT "{CLR HOME}{CRSR DOWN}{CRSR DOWN}"
1020     PRINT Z;"FOR X=";A + 1;"TO";B
1030     PRINT Z + S;"READ A: CS=CS+A: POKE X,A"
1040     PRINT Z + 2 * S;"NEXT X"
1050     Z = Z + 4 * S
1060     PRINT "GOTO 200"
1070     GOTO 800
```

Save this program as *DATAGEN* before running!!! Here's what it does:

The program generates a BASIC loader for you. You'll need to know the
starting and ending addresses of the machine language program and the
memory configuration (normally Bank 0). In addition, you choose the line
number to start, increment, etc. The first line number should be larger than
1300; otherwise the DATA generator program will be overwritten. Once
this is complete, the DELETE command erases the DATA generator
program, after which you may want to renumber the program.

C-128	C-64	MEANING
***		
208	198	Number of characters to be given by the keyboard.
842-851	631-640	Keyboard buffer (normal); 10 bytes to be given are stored in keyboard buffer .
2592	649	Maximum size of keyboard buffer (10).

Important: "Real-time" line insertion is also possible in C-64 mode, but it's a lot easier to manage in C-128 mode. When you change lines in 64 mode, all the variables are cleared. This is not the case in C-128 mode, because a special memory bank is set aside for variables (Bank 1).

The maximum size of the keyboard buffer is normally 10, which is usually sufficient. If need be, command words can be inserted in "short form" (see the back of the C-128 User's manual for abbreviations). Otherwise, the C-128 lets you change the keyboard buffer to a maximum of 20 elements. This overwrites the TAB-bitmap memory, which means that the TAB key won't work properly. The enlarged keyboard buffer covers memory locations 842 to 861. Change the size of the keyboard buffer with this command:

```
POKE 2592,20
```

CHAPTER 6

THE DATASETTE

In this chapter, we're going to show you a few neat tricks for your Datasette (or whatever compatible tape drive you may have). We imagine that most of the C-128 owners have opted for the 1571 disk drive. By the same token, if you can be patient with the tape drive's speed, it's a good, cheap alternative to a disk drive (beats having nothing for storing programs).

6.1 SOFTWARE CONTROL FOR DATASETTE

Those who use the Datasette usually don't notice that the cassette motor stops on its own when the drive is through saving or loading programs. This motor is controlled by the operating system, but can also be controlled by software (i.e., through programming). The important addresses are locations 1 (processor port) and 192 (cassette motor flag).

Try this: press the PLAY button on your recorder; the motor runs and the tape spins. Now type this in direct mode:

```
POKE 192,1:POKE1,PEEK(1) OR 32
```

The motor stops without your touching the recorder. Let's get the motor running again:

```
POKE 1, PEEK(1) AND 39:POKE 192,0
```

The key to this is the processor port, address 1. Bit 3 (CASS WRT), bit 4 (CASS SENS) and bit 5 (CASS MOTOR) of this address deal with cassette operation. To switch the motor on, the bit CASS MOTOR must be turned on.

Now you can control the cassette drive using a timing loop to create a catalog of your programs, or even set up function keys to switch the motor on and off.

6.2 SENSING THE DATASETTE KEYS

Address 1 does more! Bit 4 checks to see if a key is pressed on the Datasette, which is part of the operating system ("PRESS PLAY(&RECORD) ON TAPE" messages are controlled here). Unfortunately, the computer is unable to discern *which* Datasette key is pressed. This can be a nuisance if the user presses PLAY and forgets to press RECORD as well; the system won't catch the error.

This bit checks for the tape switches:

```
WAIT 1,16        (Wait until STOP is pressed on recorder)
WAIT 1,32,32     (Wait until a key has been pressed on the recorder)
```

We can also make the system test for RUN-STOP:

```
IF PEEK(1)=99 THEN PRINT "OOPS"
```

6.3 DOING UNUSUAL THINGS WITH THE DDR

Okay, what is a "DDR"? And what sort of "unusual things" can you do with it?

A lot, we think. The processor port is basically an I/O (Input/Output) port, handled by the CIAs. This port has six lines, three of which are dedicated to the Datasette. The lines act as both output and input; these directions are determined by the DDR (Data Direction Register) for the processor port, found at address 0. The layout:

        bit 3 : Data direction CASS WRT
        bit 4 : Data direction CASS SENS
        bit 5 : Data direction CASS MOTOR

    0 = Input
    1 = Output

CASS WRT and CASS MOTOR are output. They affect the recorder when writing to tape. CASS SENS is an input line. It checks if a tape drive key down or not.

6.4 COPY PROTECTION WITH THE DATASETTE

What happens if we change the bits in the DDR? The POKE below turns CASS SENS into an output line:

```
POKE 0,PEEK(0) OR 2^4
```

The result: CASS SENS will not register cassette status. The system will say, "PRESS PLAY(& RECORD) ON TAPE", and even if you do so, the operating system won't acknowledge "OK", or LOAD, or SAVE. Changing things back to normal is a simple matter of typing:

```
POKE 0,PEEK(0) AND NOT 2^4
```

By changing CASS WRT, we can produce a method of copy protection:

```
POKE 0, PEEK(0) AND NOT 2^3
```

The prompt will come up, the keys will be sensed, and the SAVE routine will *appear* to work...but it won't. To return to normal:

```
POKE 0,PEEK(0) OR 2^3
```

One last possibility is to alter the motor control. Re-enter:

```
POKE 0,PEEK(0) AND NOT 2^4
```

The solution to this problem:	POKE 0,PEEK(0) OR 2^4

6.5 "LO-FI" -- THE DATASETTE AS MUSIC BOX

Stereo systems and video disc players have been developed with computer interfaces built in. This means that in a few years, your stereo and video equipment will be computer controlled. Right now, some computers allow you to play audio cassettes through the computer's data system. We give you a program that does just that on the next page. A word of warning: the sound quality -- well, the word "rotten" would describe it best.

The program below manipulates the three I/O lines of the processor port. There is another, unused line between the recorder and the computer (CASS READ, the equivalent of CASS WRT). All "incoming" data goes through this line. The problem: The line doesn't end at the processor, like the other lines -- it continues on to CIA1 (putting the serial port at our disposal). So register 13 of CIA1 will have to be set:

REG 13 BIT 4:1= Signal tripped on pin FLAG

Here's the machine code listing:

```
1A00 A0 00       LDY #$00       :VOLUME 0
1A02 AD 0D DC    LDA $DC0D      :Check FLAG pin on CIA1
1A05 C9 00       CMP #$00       :No signal?
1A07 F0 02       BEQ $1A0B      :YES--go on
1A09 A0 0F       LDY #$0F       :NO--turn off volume
1A0B 8C 18 D4    STY $D418      :and SID register 24
1A0E A5 D5       LDA $D5        :Read keyboard
1A10 C9 58       CMP #$58       :88=no key pressed
1A12 F0 EC       BEQ $1A00      :No keys -- go on
1A14 60          RTS            :Return to BASIC
```

And the BASIC loader:

```
5000    FOR X = 6656 TO 6676
5010    READ A: CS = CS + A:   POKE X,A
5020    NEXT X
5030    IF CS <> 2799 THEN  PRINT  CHR$ (7);: LIST
5040    DATA 160,0,173,13,220,201,0,240,2,160,15,140
5050    DATA 24,212,165,213,201,88,240,236,96
```

Start this program with the command: SYS DEC ("1A00"). The principle of this program is simple: It looks for a signal at FLAG. If that's the case, the speaker is turned on; if not, the speaker remains off. The switching on and off occurs within the smallest loop possible in machine language and a horrible tone comes out.

If you put a music cassette into the system, it will probably sound pretty mangled; the tone is filtered as much as possible.

6.6 SAVING TO CASSETTE -- SORT OF

The SAVE command needs no introduction; you know what it is, and how it works. But what are those funny sounds made by a cassette (did you listen, using the program in the last chapter?)? The peeps are made by the CASS WRT line:

                bit 3 CASS WRT
                    1=impulse

It's fairly simple to make your own tape impulse:

```
10   REM TONES ON CASSETTE
20   PRINT "PRESS PLAY AND RECORD ON TAPE"
30   WAIT 1,32,32
40   FOR W= 1 TO 20
50   FOR K= 0 TO 20
60   POKE 1,PEEK(1) OR 8:REM IMPULSE
70   FOR T = 1 TO W:REM DELAY
80   NEXT T
90   POKE 1,PEEK(1) AND NOT 8:REM SET BACK
100 NEXT K
110 NEXT W
120 END
```

This short program saved different high and low tones to your cassette.
Use the previous program to listen to the various sounds created. It should
demonstrate the principle.

CHAPTER 7

THE KEYBOARD

7.1. KEYBOARD ASSIGNMENT

There are many ways to read the keyboard besides the BASIC commands GET and INPUT, especially for machine language programmers. In zero page location 213 ($D5) the computer stores the value of the currently pressed key. This value is not the ASCII value—it is derived from the keyboard table in the ROM of the computer.

The C-64 stores the currently pressed key in zero-page location 203 ($CB). Due to the additional keys on the C-128 the values are not always the same. Below is a chart showing what value is returned for each key pressed.

Key	Value	Key	Value
Left arrow	57	1	56
2	59	3	8
4	11	5	16
6	19	7	24
8	27	9	32
0	35	+	40
-	43	O	48
CLR HOME	51	INST DEL	0
CTRL	58	Q	62
W	9	E	14
R	17	T	22
Y	25	U	30
I	33	o	38
P	41	@	46
*	49	^(up arrow)	54
RUN-STOP	63	A	10
S	13	D	18
F	21	G	26

H	29	J	34
K	37	L	42
:	45	;	50
=	53	RETURN	1
Z	12	X	23
C	20	V	31
B	28	N	39
M	36	'	47
.	44	/	55
CRSR down	7	CRSR right	2
SPACE	60		

There are differences between the C-64 and C-128. No key pressed returns the value 88 on the C-128. On the C-64 no key returns the value 64.

The following keys are brand new on the C-128:

Help-Button	64
Tab-Button	67
ESC-Button	72
Line Feed	75

In addition to the cursor keys below the <RETURN> key (which return the same values in both machines) there are four new cursor keys. These have different values!

Cursor up	83
Cursor down	84
Cursor left	85
Cursor right	86

The C-128 also includes a numeric keypad. Just like the separate cursor keys, the values returned by the keypad keys are not equal to the values returned for the numbers on the alphanumeric keyboard. Here are the values for both keyboards on the C-128:

Key	Keyboard	Keypad
1	56	71
2	59	68
3	8	79
4	11	69
5	16	66
6	19	77
7	24	70
8	27	65
9	32	78
0	35	81
.	44	82
RETURN	1	76
+	40	73
-	43	74

The joystick of port 1 can also affect location 213 ($CD). Unfortunately this address is not useful for reading the joystick. When you push the joystick upward, the address will not change. You could use this fact to connect another keyboard to port 1.

Joystick up	88	Effect like ALT
Joystick in the middle	88	No effect
key pushed	92	Effect like shift

Joystick left	90	Effect like CTRL
Joystick right	91	
Joystick down	89	

With the following program you can simulate the BASIC 7.0 command GETKEY:

```
10 IF PEEK(213) = 88 THEN 10
20 GET A$
30 PRINT A$
40 GOTO 10
```

Of course, this command sequence in BASIC programs doesn't make much sense because the GETKEY command already exists. This program can be converted for machine language programs. In assembly language the program would be very short and could look as following:

```
Loop    LDA $D5
        CMP $58
        BEQ Loop
```

After leaving the loop the accumulator contains the value of the key pressed for further processing.

7.2. CHANGING KEY ASSIGNMENTS

Every computer programmer and user has his/her own ideas on how to use a computer. Many people became interested in computers through computer games. For this group the computer industry designed their products to be user-friendly, with easily-connected joysticks, lightpen, trackball, or paddles.

Another group of computer users are people who got involved with computers because of their jobs. The C-128 will probably be more popular with this group than was the C-64, because the C-128 can also run CP/M. CP/M is an operating system that runs on a wide variety of computers. CP/M's ability to run on many different computers has made it a very popular operating system. To expand the performance of the C-128 it would be very useful to change the key assignments, depending on the requirements of the user.

This is not as easy in the C-128 as it is in the C-64. The keyboard decoder table is located in the ROM:

64128 ($FA80) for ASCII operation

64809 ($FD29) for DIN operation (international models only)

On the international models of the C-128, two character decoding tables are included in ROM. This is to give the international models the correct foreign character sets for the countries in which they are sold. We have checked the U.S. models and the German models (DIN stands for Deutsche [German] Industry Norm). On the international models the <CAP-LOCK>

key is replaced by an <ASCII-DIN> key. When this key is pressed the operating system loads the foreign character (DIN) set into memory. Minor changes were made to the operating system to accommodate this; for more details please see the book *Commodore 128 Internals* from Abacus.

You can read the key assignments (with the monitor use the command MFFA80), but you can't change the assignments because they are in ROM. There is another way. In zero page there is an pointer to the keyboard decoder table. It is at locations 830 ($033E) and 831 ($033F). To change these values on the international models a little trick is needed. On both the U.S. and the international models you will be able to change the low-byte, but you will not be able to enter commands anymore because the keyboard will not be decoded properly.

On the international models, as soon as you change the high-byte of the pointer (at 831) you will notice that the computer has reset these locations back to their normal values.

This doesn't happen because the address is in the ROM. It is caused by the permanent check of the <ASCII-DIN> key. On the international models when the high-byte does not equal the value which is preset for the current mode, the address is reset. You can prevent the permanent check of the <ASCII-DIN> key, by setting the seventh bit of address 2757 ($0AC5).

```
POKE 2757, PEEK(2757) or 128
```

Now you can change the pointer to the decoder table on the international models. It will not reset automatically again. This is not necessary on the U.S. models.

When you alter this pointer you will no longer be able to enter any commands from the keyboard. When you push a key a character will appear but it is seldom the one you pressed. You must press the reset button to return the computer back to normal operation; not even a <RUN-STOP/RESTORE> helps. For this reason, you should copy one of the character set tables to RAM before switching. Example at 6912 ($1B00):

```
10 REM Copy and switch
20 FOR I=O TO 88
30 POKE 6912+I, PEEK(64128+I)
40 NEXT I
50 REM INTERNATIONAL MODELS ONLY:
      POKE 2757,PEEK(2757) OR 128
60 POKE 830,0
70 POKE 831,27
```

On the international models, if you had the <ASCII-DIN> key on, you would not recognize a big difference. If you started the program when the ASCII character set was activated, you will have the <CAPS-LOCK> character set, which is normal in the American version. When the <CAPS-LOCK> key is on, all letters appear as capital letters, just like the <SHIFT> or <SHIFT-LOCK> key. The difference is, the numbers appear just like before and not the upper character, obtained with <SHIFT>. If <CAPS-LOCK> is not pushed, you have the normal character set.

Now back to changing the keyboard assignments. In the previous section is a chart showing keyboard assignment values, which you can use now. Take the value of the key you would like to change and add it to 6912. In this location you store the ASCII value of the new assignment.

Example: You would like to change Y and Z. Just add these lines to the

Example: You would like to change Y and Z. Just add these lines to the previous program:

```
80 POKE 6912+12,89
90 POKE 6912+25,90
```

After the program finishes running the Y is the Z key and Z the Y. It is really that easy.

Another tip that will help you to enter machine language listings, in the form of DATA statements, faster into your computer. In the keypad is a period key. This character is useless for entering DATA statements for machine language programs. Instead of this period a comma would make entering DATA statements much easier. So we'll change the keypad, to a comma instead of the period:

```
10 REM COMMA INSTEAD POINT
20 FOR I=O TO 88
30 POKE 6912+I,PEEK(64128+I)
40 NEXT I
50 POKE 2757,PEEK(2757) OR 128
60 POKE 830,0
70 POKE 831,27
80 POKE 6994,44
```

7.3. HEX-KEYBOARD FOR THE C-128

If you work with hexadecimal numbers, then you know the problems of entering these numbers from the normal keyboard.

Above the keypad are the eight function keys. You only have to assign those with the six necessary letters. After this change you still have two keys left which are not assigned to any function. But we'll also change those. We assign those two keys to the function DEC(" and HEX$(, which are used often. Often, during programming you have only one hand free. Your second hand is busy holding books, lists and other things. For this reason, some of the letters that are reachable only with the <SHIFT> key are awkward to use. But there are still plus and minus keys which are not really necessary for entering hex-numbers. Thats why we'll assign those keys to the letters E and F.

And here is an example how you can enter hex-decimal numbers with one hand:

```
10  REM Hex-keyboard on the C-128
20  KEY 1,"A"
30  KEY 3,"B"
40  KEY 5,"C"
50  KEY 7,"D"
60  KEY 2,"E"
70  KEY 4,"F"
80  KEY 6,"PRINT DEC("+CHR$(34)
90  KEY 8,"PRINT HEX$("
100 For I=O TO 88
110 POKE 6192+I.PEEK(64128+I)
120 NEXT I
130 POKE 2757,PEEK(2757) or 128
```

```
140 POKE 6994, 32
150 POKE 6985, 69
160 POKE 6986, 70
```

You reach the letters "E" and "F" when you push the keys <SHIFT> and <F1> or <SHIFT> and <F3>, or with the plus key (E) and the minus key (F).

When you would like to convert a hexadecimal number to a decimal number you only have to push the keys <SHIFT> and <F5>. You can convert a decimal number to a hexadecimal number with SHIFT and <F7>.

7.4.SHIFT, C=, CTRL, ALT KEY ASSIGNMENTS

When you used the program where we changed the Y and Z, you probably saw, that the shifted values of these keys remain unchanged. For assignments using the <SHIFT>, the <C=> key, the <ALT> key and the <CTRL> key, there are separate tables. For the ASCII character set (U.S. models) the tables are located as follows:

64128 ($FA80)	First assignment
64217 ($FAD9)	With SHIFT
64306 ($FB32)	With COMMODORE-Key
64395 ($FB8B)	With CTRL
64128 ($FA80)	With ALT (same meaning without shift)

On the international models the C-128 has a second foreign language character set. When the <ASCII-DIN> key is pressed, you can change the keyboard assignment. Therefore you have four completely different tables, containing the keyboard decoder tables and the shift assignments. Here are the current addresses:

64809 ($FD29)	Initial value
64898 ($FD81)	With SHIFT-KEY
64987 ($FDDB)	With COMMODORE-KEY
65076 ($FE34)	With CTRL
64128 ($FA80)	With ALT

Pointers to the respective table for each of the five keys are located in zero page. On the international models there is also a pointer for the <ASCII/DIN> key:

830-831 ($033E-$033F)	Standard key press
832-833 ($0340-$0341)	With <SHIFT>
834-835 ($0342-$0343)	With Commodore (<C=>)
836-837 ($0344-$0345)	With <CTRL>
838-839 ($0346-$0347)	With <ALT>
840-841 ($0348-$0349)	With <ASCII-DIN> or <CAPS-LOCK> key

Each table has 89 bytes, equal to the 88 keys, plus the possibility that no key is pressed.

To replace two keys, you have to change the values in all four tables. The following program will do this:

```
10  REM Z and Y change
15  BANK 15
20  FOR I=O to 90*4
30  POKE 6656*I,PEEK (64128+I)
40  NEXT I
50  POKE 2757,PEEK(2757) or 128
60  REM normal table
70  POKE 6656+12,89
80  POKE 6656+25,90
90  REM Shift-Chart
100 POKE 6656+89+12,89+32
110 POKE 6656+89+25,90+32
120 REM Commodore-Chart
130 POKE 6656+2 * 89+12,183
140 POKE 6656+2 * 89+25,184
150 REM CTRL
160 POKE 6656+3 * 89+12,25
170 POKE 6656+3 * 89+25,26
180 REM Change pointer
190 POKE 830,0
200 POKE 831,26
210 POKE 832,89
220 POKE 833,26
230 POKE 834,89 * 2
240 POKE 835,26
250 POKE 836,11
260 POKE 837,27
```

Now you can change the shifted key assignments to anything you want.
The new key assignment does not have to be at address 6656. Remember,
you also have to change the pointer (830 - 841).

7.5. THE AUXILIARY KEYS

The computer needs extra keys to make it possible for a key to have more than one value. The C-64 had three extra keys: <SHIFT> (both <SHIFT> and <SHIFT LOCK> have the same function), <C=> and <CTRL>.

The C-128 has these, as well as three additional keys: <ESC>, <ALT> and the <CAPS-LOCK> (<ASCII-DI> on the international models).

ESC means escape. This key is not a new invention from Commodore. It has been used for many years in other computers. With the <ESC> key on the C-128 you can do functions like switching from the 40 to the 80 column screen. Every key has a special function in combination with the <ESC> key. But <ESC> is different than the <SHIFT>, <C=> and <CTRL> keyss: <ESC> and another key are not pressed simultaneously, but one after each other.

7.5.1. USING THE AUXILIARY KEYS

The auxiliary keys can be read at memory location 211 ($D3). If one of the <SHIFT> keys or <SHIFT-LOCK> key is pressed, the first bit is set. With the <C=> key the second bit is set. The third bit is for <CTRL>, and the fourth for <ALT>. The next bit is set by pressing the <CAP-LOCK> (<ASCII-DIN>) key. Because these keys can be pressed at the same time, there are 31 possible combinations. The following table shows a few of

those possibilities. It is not complete and only intended as an example.
Once you understand the principle, a complete table is not necessary.

0 - No Extra keys	1 - SHIFT
2 - COMMODORE - KEY	3 - SHIFT + COMMODORE
4 - CTRL - KEY	5 - SHIFT + CTRL
8 - ALT	10 - ALT + COMMODORE
15 - SHIFT+COMMODORE+CTRL+ALT	16 - CAPS LOCK
	(ASCII/DIN-KEY)

7.6. EIGHT ADDITIONAL FUNCTION KEYS

When the eight existing function keys are not enough, the following
program will solve your problems.

To any of the new function keys you can assign text that is sixteen
characters long, similar to the KEY command, and you can enter all the
control commands. You get the additional function keys with the <ALT>
key. You get the first function key, when you press ALT only, the second
with <ALT> and <SHIFT>. The <C=> key and <CTRL> key in
combination with <ALT> key activates the third and fourth. As a
by-product you get four more function keys but those are much harder to
produce. You would have to push several extra keys and <ALT> key at the
same time.

The following BASIC loader is a program that lets you assign the eight new
<ALT> function keys. You can't edit the text for the extra function keys

directly on the screen. Only after you are finished entering the text will it be
displayed. You are then asked if everything is correct. When you program
your own use for the <ALT> key you can use the same principles as we did
in the following machine language program.

```
10       REM  8 EXTRA FUNCTION KEYS
20       FOR I = 5120 TO 5190
30       READ A
40       S = S + A
45       POKE I,A
50       IF A <>  PEEK (I) THEN  PRINT A,I, PEEK (I)
60       NEXT I
70       IF S <  > 7375 THEN BEGIN
80       PRINT "?ERROR IN DATA   "
90       END
100      BEND
110      BANK 0:  SYS 5120
120      DATA 120,169,13,141,20,3,169,20,141
130      DATA 21,3,88,96,72,152,72,165
140      DATA 211,168,41,8,240,29,152,205
150      DATA 96,20,240,23,141,96,20,10
160      DATA 10,10,10,168,185,0,20,240
170      DATA 13,201,13,240,15,32,210,255
180      DATA 200,208,241,140,96,20,104,168
190      DATA 104,76,101,250,141,74,3,169
200      DATA 1,133,208,76,55,20
210      REM  INPUT OF THE FUNCTION KEYS
220      FOR I = 0 TO 7
230      B$ = "               ":  REM  15 SPACES
240      PRINT "ALT-";I + 1
250      PRINT "INPUT TEXT:  END WITH  LINE FEED"
260      FOR J = 0 TO 14
270      GET  KEY A$
280      IF A$ =  CHR$ (10) THEN 330
290      IF A$ =  CHR$ (13) THEN 330
300      MID$ (B$,J + 1,1) = A$
310      POKE 5248 + J + I * 16, ASC (A$)
320      NEXT J
330      POKE 5248 + J + I * 16,0
340      PRINT B$
350      INPUT "ALL OK  (Y/N)";A$
```

```
360     IF A$ = "N" THEN 230
370     NEXT I
```

Here is the machine language portion of the above routine:

```
1400    78          SEI             ;Prevents Interrupt
1401    A9 OD       LDA #$OD        ;Sets Interrupt vector
1403    8D 14 03    STA $0341
1406    A9 14       LDA #$14
1408    8D 15 03    STA $0315
140B    58          CLI             ;Permit IRQ
140C    60          RTS             ;Back to Basic
140D    48          PHA             ;Accumulator on Stack
140E    98          TYA             ;Y-Register in Accu.
140F    48          PHA             ;Accumulator on Stack
1410    A5 D3       LDA $D3         ;Flag for ALT
1412    A8          TAY             ;Accu. in Y Register
1413    29 08       AND #$08        ;Bit 3 set?
1415    FO 1D       BEQ $1434       ;No, then $1434
1417    98          TYA             ;Value back in Accu.
1418    CD 60 14    CMP $1460       ;Previous Key ALT ?
141B    FO 17       BEQ $1434       ;Yes, then $1434
141D    8D 60 14    STA $1460       ;Stores 8
1420    OA          ASL             ;Move four Bits
1421    OA          ASL             ;To the Left
1422    OA          ASL
1423    OA          ASL
1424    A8          TAY             ;Accu. in Y register
1425    B9 00 14    LDA$1400,Y;Character
1428    FO OD       BEQ $1437       ;$1437 whenzero
142A    C9 OD       CMP #$OD        ;Return ?
142C    FO OF       BEQ $143D       ;Yes, then $143D
142E    20 D2 FF    JSR $FFD2       ;Give out Character
1431    C8          INY
1432    DO F1       BNE $1425
1434    8C 60 14    STY $1460       ;Stores Helpbutton
1437    68          PLA             ;Accumulator from Stack
1438    A8          TAY             ;Accu. to Y Register
1439    68          PLA             ;Accumulator from Stack
143A    4C 65 FA    GMP $FA65       ;To normal Interrupt
143D    8D 4A 03    STA $034A       ;Return in Key Buffer
1440    A9 01       LDA #$01
```

```
1442     85 D0      STA $D0
1444     4c 37 14   JMP $1437
```

7.7. KEYBOARD BEEP

Here is another little program that gives your C-128 programs a more
professional appearance: press any key and a low volume beep will sound.

The program changes the IRQ vector, so it reacts very fast to every key
press. For this reason it is not written in BASIC, but you can enter it in
your computer with the BASIC loader. To make programing easier your
computer will also give out a different tone whenever the <RETURN> key
is pressed. Below is the assembly language listing for those of you who are
familiar with machine language.

```
1400 A9 FF       LDA #$FF      ; Set Value For
1402 8D 06 D4    STA $D406     ; the Beeptone
1405 8D 18 D4    STA $D418     ;
1408 A9 09       LDA #$09
140A 8D 05 D4    STA $D405
140D 78          SEI           ; Prevents Interrupt
140E A9 1A       LDA #$1A
1410 8D 14 03    STA $0314     ; IRQ-Vector open
1413 A9 14       LDA #$14      ; Beep-Routine

1415 8D 15 03    STA $0315     ; set
1418 58          CLI           ; Permits Interrupt
1419 60          RTS           ; Back in BASIC
141A 48          PHA           ; Accu. on Stack
141B A5 D5       LDA $D5       ; Val. pushed key
141D C9 58       CMP #$58      ; key pushed?
141F F0 24       BEQ $1443     ; Yes
1421 C9 4C       CMP #$4C      ; RETURN?
```

```
1421 C9 4C        CMP #$4C      ; RETURN?
1423 D0 0D        BNE $1431     ; no, then $1431.
1425 A9 67        LDA #$67      ; stores Frequences.
1427 BD 00 D4     STA $D400     ; Tone by RETURN
142A A9 11        LDA #$11
142C 8D 01 D4     STA $D401
142F D0 14        BNE $1445
1431 C9 01        CMP #$01      ; RETURN key?
1433 F0 F0        BEQ $1425     ; Yes, then $1425.
1435 A9 67        LDA #$67      ; set Frequence for
1437 8D 01 D4     STA $D401     ; the Beeptone
143A A9 21        LDA #$21
143C 8D 00 D4     STA $D400
143F A9 11        LDA #$11      ; Waveform
1441 D0 02        BNE $1445     ; Skip Next Line
1443 A9 00        LDA #$00      ; Waveform, when no
                                ;   key pushed
1445 8D 04 D4     STA $D404     ; Store Waveform
1448 68           PLA           ; Accum. from Stack
144A 4C 65 FA     JMP $FA65     ; Normal IRQ
```

Here is the BASIC loader:

```
10     REM  KEY SOUND
20     FOR I = 5120 TO 5195
30     READ A
40     S = S + A
50     POKE I,A
60     NEXT I
70     IF S <  > 8932 THEN BEGIN
80     PRINT "?ERROR{SPACE}IN{SPACE}DATA"
90     END
100     BEND
110     SYS 5120
120     DATA 169,255,141,6,212,141,24,212
130     DATA 169,9,141,5,212,120,169,26
140     DATA 141,20,3,169,20,141,21,3
150     DATA 88,96,72,165,213,201,88,240
160     DATA 34,201,76,208,12,169,103,141
170     DATA 0,212,169,17,141,1,212,208
```

```
180     DATA 20,201,1,240,240,169,103,141
190     DATA 1,212,169,33,141,0,212,169
200     DATA 17,208,2,169,0,141,4,212
210     DATA 104,76,101,250
```

7.8. PROGRAM PAUSE

With this routine you can assign a program pause function to any key, you
can stop program execution with the key of your choice. You can answer
the door or the telephone without missing any computing.

If you would like to assign the program pause function to a key other than
the <NO-SCROLL> key, you have to add the following POKE commands
to the end of the BASIC loader:

```
POKE  5134,  N
POKE  5140,  N
```

The parameter N must contain the value of the key you choose. You can
find the exact values in the chapter 7.1.

The interrupted program resumes when you press any other key. This key
stays in the keyboard buffer and is read by the next input statement.

```
10     REM  PAUSE-FUNCTION
20     FOR I = 5120 TO 5165
30     READ A
40     S = S + A
50     POKE I,A
```

```
60      NEXT
70      IF S < > 5361 THEN BEGIN
80      PRINT "?ERROR{SPACE}IN{SPACE}DATA"
90      END
100     BEND
110     SYS 5120
140     DATA 169,11,141,8,3,169,20,141
150     DATA 9,3,96,165,212,201,87,208
160     DATA 10,165,212,201,87,240,250,201
170     DATA 88,240,246,169,15,133,2,169
180     DATA 74,133,3,169,162,133,4,169
190     DATA 0,133,5,76,227,2
```

The routine in machine language:

```
1400 A9 0B      LDA #$0B        : Changes Vector
1402 8D 08 03   STA $0308       ; For "execute
1405 A9 14      LDA #$14        ; next BASIC-Line"
1407 8D 09 03   STA $0309
140A 60         RTS             ; Back to BASIC
140B A5 D4      LDA $D4         ; Value of Key
140D C9 40      CMP #$57        ; NO SCROLL?
140F D0 0A      BNE $141B       ; No
1411 A5 D4      LDA $D4         ; Value of Key
1413 C9 40      CMP #$57        ; NO SCROLL?
1415 F0 FA      BEQ $1411       ; Yes, then wait
1417 C9 58      CMP #$58        ; No Key?
1419 F0 F6      BEQ $1411       ; Yes, then wait
141B A9 0F      LDA #$0F        ; Next BASIC-Line
141D 85 02      STA $02         ; execute
141F A9 4E      LDA #$4A
1421 85 03      STA $03
1423 A9 A2      LDA #$A2
1425 85 04      STA $04
1427 A9 00      LDA #$00
1429 85 05      STA $05
142B 4C E3 02   JMP $02E3
```

7.9. HELP & RUN/STOP KEY ASSIGNMENT

The C-128 has a total of ten function keys, that you can assign yourself. In addition to the eight function keys above the numeric keypad, there are two more: one of them is the <HELP> key, which is actually function key ten. You can reach the ninth function key with the <SHIFT> and <RUN-STOP> key combination. This key is assigned with

```
DLOAD"*
RUN
```

These lines load the first program from the disk drive and then run the program. This text can be changed, but not with the KEY Command. If you enter KEY 9 or KEY 10 the computer will print out " ? ILLEGAL QUANTITY ERROR ".

But a little program can take care of that problem:

```
10    REM  FUNCTION KEY  9 + 10
20    REM  [SHIFT] RUN/STOP + HELP
30    FOR I = 4096 TO 4103
40    A = A +  PEEK (I)
50    NEXT I
60    PRINT "^ = RETURN"
70    PRINT  CHR$ (27);"F"
80    FOR I = 0 TO 1
90    PRINT "FUNCTION KEY # "9 + I
110   GET  KEY B$
120   IF B$ <  >  CHR$ (13) THEN BEGIN
130   PRINT B$;
140   B =  ASC (B$)
150   IF B = 94 THEN B = 13
160   POKE 4106 + A + Z,B
```

```
170    Z = Z + 1
180    IF A + Z + 4106 > 4351 THEN    END
190    GOTO 110
200    BEND
210    PRINT
220    POKE 4104 + I,Z
230    A = A + Z
240    Z = 0
250    NEXT I
```

With this program you can change the assignment of these two keys. If you'd like to execute a <RETURN> (CHR$(13)) after the text, you have to enter an up arrow (↑). To make it possible to enter commas we used the GET command.

After minor changes, this program can be also used to change the assignment of the other function keys. This would be very useful for function key assignments with text of more than 128 characters. In this case you would obtain an error using the KEY command.

The assignment of the function keys is in memory at 4096 ($1000) to 4AA2 ($1100). In the first ten bytes, the length of the function key text is stored. With these values you can find out the start address of the text. When you add the first five bytes to each other, you get the start address to the text of F6. You can assign a total of 245 characters to the 10 function keys. The program will not allow you to enter a longer text.

Of course you can use different control characters other than <RETURN>. You can enter these directly. Example: If you like to scroll up your screen ten times you just push the <ESC> and the <W> key 10 times.

If you entered a wrong character you should not use the <INST-DEL> key. This key seems to work alright, but the entering of the <INST-DEL> key will then be stored in the function key definition.

CHAPTER 8

COMMAND EXTENSIONS

After you switch on the C-128 it displays the following message:

```
COMMODORE BASIC V7.0 122365 BYTES FREE
    (C)1985 COMMODORE ELECTRONICS, LTD.
         (C)1977 MICROSOFT CORP.
           ALL RIGHTS RESERVED
```

Microsoft developed the popular version of BASIC called *MBASIC* that's widely used on CP/M computers. *MBASIC* has a large command set; perhaps this is why the BASIC 7.0 of the C-128 has so many commands. BASIC V7.0 is upward compatible to the BASIC V2.0, V4.0 and V3.5. The V2.0 version is the grandfather of the other BASICs; the VIC-20 and the C-64 contain BASIC V2.0. BASIC V4.0 is used in the large Commodore computers, such as the 8000 series. Commands for the disk drives were added to the commands of BASIC V2.0 (for example, DIRECTORY).

The next BASIC version, BASIC V3.5, is for the C-16, C-116 (available in Europe) and the Plus/4 computers. BASIC V3.5 contained many new graphic commands. Programming aids and a machine language monitor are also included in V3.5

The C-128 features BASIC V7.0. Even more commands have been added, such as sprite control, music programing (limited in version V3.5) and disk commands. And there is another convenient option: the command GO 64.

This command turns the C-128 into a C-64 .

Even with all the new commands, you'll find that more are required. How about PRINT AT?, or POP?, or GOTO X? and RESTORE X?. We easily could continue this list. As a frequent programmer you'll rely on several helpful routines, such as APPEND. What then? You'd usually call them with a SYS and some values behind it. But how many addresses can you remember, and how understandable is a program when it's full SYS commands?

Luckily it's easy to insert new commands into the operating systems of Commodore computers. We use the routine called CHRGET (CHRGET means CHaRacter + GET) to accomplish this small miracle.

8.1. WHAT IS THE CHRGET ROUTINE ?

When you turn on the C-128 the CHRGET routine is copied from the ROM to the RAM. We will explain that later. Right now we'll deal with the function of the CHRGET routine.

With the CHRGET routine, the computer takes a character from the BASIC text, meaning from the program memory or from the BASIC input buffer. The BASIC interpreter always jumps to the CHRGET routine to get the next character. Lets have a look at the CHRGET routine for the C-64:

```
0073        INC   $7A
0075        BNE   $0079
0077        INC   $7B
```

```
0079        LDA     $HHLL
007C        CMP     #$3A
007E        BCS     $008A
0080        CMP     #$20
0082        BEQ     $0073
0084        SEC
0085        SBC     #$30
0087        SEC
0088        SBC     #$D0
008A        RTS
```

The first three instructions increment the value of the text pointer. The least significant byte of the pointer is incremented. But if there is a carry (meaning greater than 255), then the most significant byte of the pointer is also incremented. When you look at the address of the pointer (called $HHLL in the above routine) you will notice it is located within the CHRGET routine. Now the ROM - RAM copy procedure makes sense: the routine changes itself!

 The actual value of $HHLL is the pointer to a location within the BASIC program text. The pointer is called TXTPTR and is actually a vector at $007A. The CHRGET routine loads the accumulator (LDA instruction at address $0079) with the next character of BASIC text pointed to by TXTPTR.

This character is checked in several ways.   First the character will be compared with the ASCII value for the semi-colon. The routine returns when the character is larger or equal to this value. If the character is the semi-colon, the zero-flag becomes set , in addition to the carry-flag. If the character number is smaller, the tests continue. The first test checks to see if the character is a space character. If so, the next character will be examined. In effect, space characters are ignored (PRINTX has the same

effect as PRINT X). The two next commands check to see if the character
is a number between 0 - 9.

The CHRGET routine of the C-128 has been changed:

```
0380    INC    $3D
0382    BNE    $0386
0384    INC    $3E
0386    STA    $FF01
0389    LDY    #$00
038B    LDA    ($3D), Y
038D    STA    $FF03
0390    CMP    #$3A
0392    BCS    $039E
0394    CMP    #$20
0396    BEQ    $0380
0398    SEC
0399    SBC    #$30
039B    SEC
039C    SBC    #$D0
039E    RTS
```

The first three instructions increment a pointer again. This pointer is not
within the CHRGET routine anymore, but in zero page. The next
instruction assures that the computer takes this information from the correct
bank. This instruction is similar to the BASIC command BANK 0. RAM
Bank 0 is always activated. That guarantees that the program can use the
full 64K of the RAM in Bank 0 (minus the first few pages that are used by
the system).

The next two commands instructions retrieve a character from the BASIC
text. Because the Y register is used as an offset, it must be set to zero first.

The instruction at address $038D switches the banks back again. This machine language instruction is equivalent to the BASIC command BANK 14, which switches on BASIC interpreter, character generator, and RAM Bank 0.

The following instructions are just like the C-64's, meaning the check procedure for semi-colon, space character, etc.

A last word on the CHRGET routine: once in a while the operating system jumps to the CHRGET routine at address $0386 ($0079 in the C-64). Then it's called CHRGOT. You will also get a character, but the pointer is not incremented. The last character will be read.

8.2. CHANGING THE CHRGET ROUTINE

Here we limit our discussion to the C-128, because there is enough literature available on how to change the routine on the C-64. To insert new commands you have to change the CHRGET routine--but where do you do that? Theoretically you could do it anywhere, but only two solutions are practical:

a) Each time you get a character, a certain function will be executed.

b) A new command must be inserted.

In a) you want to change the CHRGET routine at the start. Here is an example. Enter the monitor and type in the following assembler listing:

```
0380  JSR  $0B00
0383  NOP
0384  NOP
0385  NOP
- - - - - - - - - - - - - -
0B00  INC  $3D
0B02  BNE  $0B06
0B04  INC  $3E
0B06  LDA  #$00
0B08  STA  $FF00
0B0B  LDA  $D020
0B0E  EOR  #$FF
0B10  STA  $D020
0B13  RTS
```

Leave the monitor with the "X" command, type in a character and press the <RETURN> key. The border color will change (the border color of the forty column screen, because we are manipulating the VIC chip). Let's have a closer look at the listing.

It has two parts. Part one is located in the CHRGET routine and alters the routine itself. When you enter a character now, the computer will call a subroutine at $0B00. This subroutine constitutes part two. Here, it continues the first part of the CHRGET routine that was replaced by the first part. Then the I/O is switched on to gain access to the VIC chip (Bit 0 is responsible for this; see Chapter 9, "Banking"). The access to the VIC chip occurs with the next three instructions. Here we change the border color. The bank that was on before the called routine switches on again. Finally, you return to the CHRGET routine with a RTS.

You have to remember one thing: the functions performed by the CHRGET routine must be kept intact. If any section is missing, the operating system will not function properly anymore. For example, the system will crash if you leave out the instructions in the second part of the assembler listing that raise the indicator in the CHRGET - routine.

Very seldom are commands one character in length. Usually you would like an action performed only if several characters are entered. This character sequence becomes the new command.

The CIIRGET routine can accomplish this task. Enter the following assembler listing (you should reset the computer before entering the listing):

```
0380    INC    $3D
0382    BNE    $0386
0384    INC    $3E
0386    STA    $FF01
0389    LDY    #$00
038B    LDA    ($3D), Y
038D    JMP    $0B00
0390    STA    $FF03
0393    NOP
- - - - - - - - - - - - - - -
0B00    CMP    #$FF
0B02    BNE    $0B14
0B04    LDA    #$00
0B06    STA    $FF00
0B09    LDA    $D020
0B0C    EOR    #$FF
0B0E    STA    $D020
0B11    JMP    $0380
0B14    CMP    #$3A
0B16    BCS    $0B1B
0B18    JMP    $0390
0B1B    STA    $FF03
0B1E    RTS
```

This time the CHRGET routine was changed at address $038D. There we jump to address $0B00 (this time not JSR, but JMP). The instruction at address $0390 (STA $FF03) was taken from the old CHRGET routine. The NOP instruction assigns the free byte in the CHRGET routine. Now to the part after address $0B00:

First the character read is compared with the value $FF (255). This value is the token for Pi (π). If the character is not Pi (π), you continue from address $0B14. There the CHRGET routine continues. First the character is compared with that of the semi-colon. If it is larger, Bank 14 will be activated (just like the CHRGET routine); then it will jump to the address where the CHRGET routine was called. If the ASCII value of the character is smaller than the value of the semi-colon, it continues with the JMP instruction to the normal CHRGET routine.

Let's imagine the entered character was Pi (π). In this case you continue the program at address $0B04. Here, Bank 15 switches on to have access to the I/O (in this case the VIC). Then, like the other routine, the value for the screen border is inverted. Then there's the usual jump back to the CHRGET routine, to read the next character.

Now enter a Pi (π) and press the RETURN key. The border color of the forty column screen will change. When you enter Pi (π) again, the frame color goes back to normal.

Contain your curiosity and don't experiment with the Pi (π) character (for example, what happens when you enter it in a program line). First, enter the following assembler listing:

```
0380      INC       $3D
0382      BNE       $0386
0384      INC       $3E
0386      STA       $FF01
0389      LDY       #$00
038B      LDA       ($3D), Y
038D      JMP       $0B00
0390      STA       $FF03
0393      NOP
- - - - - - - - - - - - - - -
0B00      CMP       #$FF
0B02      BNE       $0B14
0B04      LDA       #$00
0B06      STA       $FF00
0B09      LDA       $D020
0B0C      EOR       #$FF
0B0E      STA       $D020
0B11      JMP       $0380
0B14      CMP       #$88
0B16      BNE       $0B28
0B18      LDA       #$00
0B1A      STA       $FF00
0B1D      LDA       #$00
0B20      EOR       #$FF
0B22      STA       $D021
0B25      JMP       $0380
0B28      CMP       #$3A
0B2A      BCS       $0B2F
0B2C      JMP       $0390
0B2F      STA       $FF03
0B32      RTS
```

Two new commands are inserted by this listing:

a) Pi (π): Here you invert the value for the border color, just like in
   the previous routine.

b) LET: This command inverts the value for the background color.

8.3. THE "BEHAVIOR" OF THE NEW COMMANDS

Enter the character Pi (π) with a line number and you will see that the command will be executed immediately. It will not be carried out in the program. Now try out the same with the command LET. The command will not be executed right away, but will be executed in a program RUN. As you can see the computer can distinguish between normal and new BASIC commands.

Now enter Pi (π) in a line again, but type in a semi-colon at the start of the line. Again, the command will be executed immediately, but the line will be maintained. That also works when you insert new commands between old commands. Enter the semi-colon and the command LET in the line. In this case you also maintain the line, and when you start the program the border and background color will change. Try the following line:

```
10 LET GOTO 10
```

Even though it looks wrong, it functions well: the value for the background color will change quickly (this effect is really interesting).

That works in the following format also:

```
10 GOTO LET 10
```

This works because the interpretation of the BASIC lines will go to the (changed) CHRGET routine. The token for GOTO will be read first. Because this value does not equal one of the values of the new commands, it jumps back from the character analysis and branchs to the GOTO command. There it will jump to the CHRGET routine again, to get the line number. But this time the character equals the value of the new command, which is $88 for LET. So, the color is changed and then jumped back to the CHRGET routine. There the next character, the number 1, is read and jumps back to the GOTO command. The command LET is executed but otherwise it is ignored. Of course, that works behind any other command. But there are some limitations:

a) The new command cannot be in other commands. The following example does not work:

```
10 GO LET TO 10
```

That is because GOTO becomes changed into a token first. In this case the GOTO command will not be identified, so it won't get changed to a token. But you can place the new command in numbers:

```
10 A=100LET0
20 PRINT A
```

Here A receives the value 1000.

b) The new command is not identified in strings.

```
10 PRINT "LET"
```

will print LET without changing the background color.

8.4. SEVERAL ADDITIONAL COMMANDS

If you want to add more commands, the listing above would be too tedious.
If you wanted to check for every new command, the command extension
would grow too large.   There is an easier method; as follows:

```
0380      INC      $3D
0382      BNE      $0386
0384      INC      $3E
0386      STA      $FF01
0389      LDY      #$00
038B      LDA      ($3D), Y
038D      JMP      $0B00
0390      STA      $FF03
0393      NOP
- - - - - - - - - - - - - - -
0B00      LDY      #$03
0B02      DEY
0B03      BMI      $0B0C
0B05      CMP      $0B23, Y
0B08      BEQ      $0B17
0B0A      BNE      $0B02
0B0C      CMP      #$3A
0B0E      BCS      $0B13
0B10      JMP      $0390
0B13      STA      $FF03
0B16      RTS
0B17      TYA
0B18      ASL
0B19      TAY
0B1A      LDA      $0B27, Y
0B1D      PHA
0B1E      LDA      $0B26, Y
0B21      PHA
0B22      RTS
0B23      $40,     $88,    $FF

0B26      $2B,     $0B
0B28      $43,     $0B
```

```
0B2A     $53,    $0B

0B2C     LDA     #$00
0B2E     STA     $FF00
0B31     LDA     $D020
0B34     EOR     #$FF
0B36     STA     $D020
0B39     LDA     $D021
0B3C     EOR     #$FF
0B3E     STA     $D021
0B41     JMP     $0380
0B44     LDA     $D021
0B46     STA     $FF00
0B49     LDA     $D021
0B4C     EOR     #$FF
0B4D     STA     $D021
0B51     JMP     $0380
0B54     LDA     #$00
0B56     STA     $FF00
0B59     LDA     $D020
0B5C     EOR     #$FF
0B5E     STA     $D020
0B61     JMP     $0380
```

In the part after $0B00 three commands are defined:

    a) Pi (π): Functions like above

    b) LET: Functions like above

    c) @ = Pi (π) and LET

The principles are easy to understand. The codes of the new commands are stored in a table, and the addresses where the commands should be executed in another table. Take a close look at the listing again:

$0B00:   Here you load the number of new commands in the X-register.

$0B02:   Decrement by one.

$0B03:   When all commands are carried out you jump to address $0B0C.

This BRANCH command also checks if the X-register contains the value zero (you also check if X=2).

$0B05: Here the entered character is compared with a byte from table $0B23 - $0B25. This table contains the values for the new commands.

$0B08: Here you jump to address $0B17 when the entered character is equal with one of the new commands.

$0B0A: If it was not equal, jump to $0B02 and compare the entered character with the next command.

$0B0C: You continue with this address when the entered character does not equal any of the new commands. At address $0B16 the routine is the same as in the normal CHRGET - Routine.

$0B17: You continue here when the entered character was equal with one command. The number of the command (0 - 2) will be placed in the X-register,

$0B18: Multiply by two

$0B19: and place back in the X-register again.

$0B1A: Here is the high-byte of the address where the new command starts, pulled in from the accumulator.

$0B1D: Stored on the stack.

$0B1E: Here you get the accompanying low-byte.

$0B21: And also stored on the stack.

You can see for yourself that with the separate X register values, the following low/high-bytes become stored on the stack:

X-Reg.	Low - Byte	High - Byte	Command
0	$2B	$0B	@
1	$43	$0B	LET
2	$53	$0B	Pi

This address must always show one byte below the address where the routine really starts. So the command LET starts not at $0B43, but at $0B44. The reason for this is in the next command:

$0B22:   Here is the return from the subroutine. But from which subroutine? $0B00 was called with JMP, and not with JSR. Now by RTS the jump address is called from the stack; first the low-byte, then the high-byte. One address was stored in the stack by the previous instructions, and called in the program counter. This is incremented to get the next command. That is why the address had to be one byte lower than the correct address. You fool the computer, because you tell it, that a JSR instruction brought it to address $0B22 (which is before the start of the respective command).

$0B23 - $0B25:   Table with codes of new commands

$0B26 - $0B2B: Table with addresses of new commands (-1!)

The new commands, which start at $0B2C, will not be explained again.

You shouldn't think you can use only commands of one byte lengths, or commands that already exist. Of course you can use your own longer commands. The length of these commands can be different. When you examine the three tables, please notice that the first contains start addresses of the strings which are to be compared, the second contains those strings, and the third has the addresses of the commands.

And here's a last tip; always place an identifying mark in front of your commands, such as @. That makes it easier to tell your own commands from the commands of the Interpreter. This will make your work easier and faster.

CHAPTER 9

BANKING

9.1. THEORETICAL BASICS

We don't want to write a book about theory, but you should know some of the basics about memory management.

A few years ago the VIC-20 standard version had only 5K of RAM. It had 3583 Bytes available for BASIC programs. It had a 20KByte of ROM, which was extendable to 32K RAM and 24K ROM. Together you had 32K + 24K = 56K memory available. This could be addressed with the 6502 processor,without any problems, because it had 16 address lines available which allows for access to $2^{16} = 65536 = 64K$ of memory.

In a short time memory became so inexpensive that computers could be packed with memory and still remain within the price range of home computers. But how was the additional memory supposed to be addressed? To install a CPU with more than 16 address lines would result in an excessive price increase.

Engineers worked out three methods to use more memory than can be addressed. For C-128 owners only one of these methods is interesting—it's called **BANKING** or **BANK SWITCHING**. In this method, memory chips are installed "above each other" , which contain the total amount of addressable memory. This means that two memory banks are located in the exact same address range. But only one memory bank is particular bank, you can electronically (under program control) switch between those banks. This makes it very easy for the user, but creates a problem for the manufacturer of the computer system.

If, after the bank switching, the program returns to the wrong bank, and hence the incorrect program code, the computer will "hang up". It would be possible to switch only a certain range (for example, the operating system) instead of the total memory range. But that would mean a loss in memory size again. There is a possibility to switch the whole memory with an easy hardware solution (just like in the C-64, when you read the address $A000, then you read from the ROM, but when you write at address $A000 you write in the RAM).

This is enough theory on bank switching and memory management. Let's return to the C-128 memory management.

9.2. BANKING WITH THE C-128

The Commodore advertisments for the C-128 state that it has 128K Bytes RAM (expandable to 512K Bytes) and 48K Bytes of ROM. How can this be possible if the microprocessor can only access 64K bytes at one time? The memory is overlayed and the proper memory bank is selected when necessary. The picture on the next page should clarify this.

But how is the memory management accomplished?

If you examine the memory diagram you will notice that the C-128 uses banking somewhat like the C-64 (the C-128 contains more overlayed memory banks. To manage this big mess, you need an additional integrated circuit. In the C-64 this was the AM (Address Manager). Because Commodore owns a company that makes integrated circuits (MOS Technology), they quickly designed a new integrated circuit called MMU 8722 (Memory Management Unit). The MMU controls which bank is currently accessed and makes sure that the computer always calls the information from the right bank.

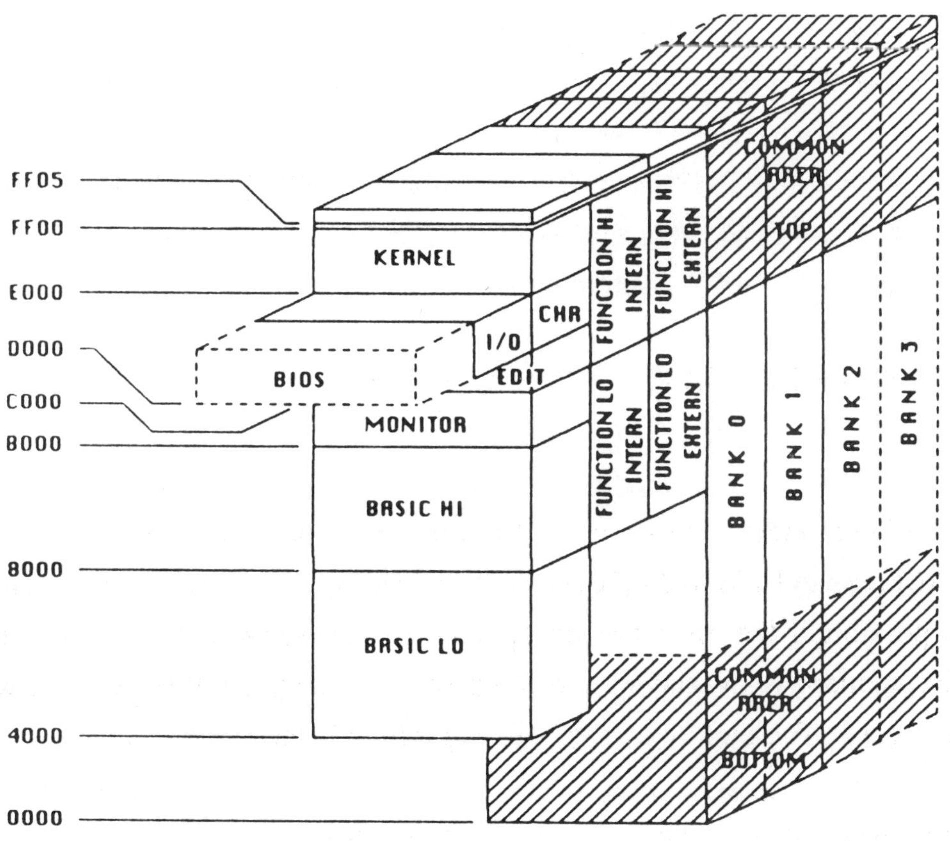

9.3. SWITCHING THE BANKS WITH THE MMU

To switch the banks you use only one register of the MMU, register 0. It is called the CR (Configuration Register). The bits have the following function:

Bit	Function
0	Selects the range $D000 - $E000 :
	$\quad$ 0 = I/0 $\qquad\qquad$ 1 = ROM / RAM
1	Selects the range $4000 - $7FFF :
	$\quad$ 0 = ROM $\qquad\qquad$ 1 = RAM
2 & 3	Selects the range $8000 - $BFFF :
	$\quad$ 00 = System ROM $\qquad$ 01 = internal function ROM
	$\quad$ 10 = external function ROM $\quad$ 11 = RAM
4 & 5	Selects the range $C000 - $FFFF :
	$\quad$ 00 = System ROM $\qquad$ 01 = internal function ROM
	$\quad$ 10 = external function ROM $\quad$ 11 = RAM
6 & 7	Selects the RAM - Memory :
	$\quad$ 00 = RAM - Bank 0 $\qquad$ 01 = RAM - Bank 1
	$\quad$ 10 = RAM - Bank 2 $\qquad$ 11 = RAM - Bank 3

Here are some further explanations:

a) Bits 4 and 5 are dependent on bit 0. This means when bits 4 and 5 are set and 0 is not, then the area from $C000 - $FFFF is not completely RAM. From $D000 - $E000 is the I/O (Input/Output). RAM would be there, when Bit 0 would be set to 1. If Bit 0 is 0, the I/O is switched on independently of bits 4 and 5. But bits 4 and 5 control the memory layout from $C000 - $FFFF.

b)   In the present versions of the C-128 bits 6 & 7 make sense in only the first two modes because the RAM Banks 2 & 3 are not available yet.

c)   In the area from $FF00 - $FF04 the system memory is located, independent from this register. The first of these five bytes ($FF00) is register 0 of the MMU. You are probably wondering why. The answer is very simple. Imagine you have the I/O switched off, for example, to access to the character generator. Now you would like to turn on the I/O, to change the screen color, but how do you switch it back on? The registers of the MMU are also in the I/O (excuse us for holding that information back so long): from $D500 - $D50B! Now the memory cell $FF00 takes action. Because this register has the same function as register 0 you can switch the I/O back on.

Because banking wouldn't be very user friendly if it could only be done using the registers of the MMU, the programmers of the BASIC interpreter implemented a new command: the BANK command. The SYNTAX is as follows:


```
BANK nr
```


The `nr` is a number from 0 to 15 that activates the respective memory configuration. On the next page is a chart showing the different memory configurations of each bank.

Nr:	Contents of $FF00	Memory Configuration
0	$3F = %00111111	RAM - Bank 0
1	$7F = %01111111	RAM - Bank 1
2	$BF = %10111111	RAM - Bank 2
3	$FF = %11111111	RAM - Bank 3
4	$16 = %00010110	Function - ROM internal, with RAM - Bank 0 and I/O
5	$56 = %01010110	Like above, but RAM - Bank 1
6	$96 = %10010110	Like above, but RAM - Bank 2
7	$D6 = %11010110	Like above, but RAM - Bank 3
8	$2A = %00101010	Function - ROM external, with RAM - Bank 0 and I/O
9	$6A = %01101010	Like above, but RAM - Bank 1
10	$AA = %10101010	Like above, but RAM - Bank 2
11	$EA = %11101010	Like above, but RAM - Bank 3
12	$06 = %00000110	Function - ROM internal low , with Kernal, RAM - Bank 0 and I/O
13	$0A = %00001010	Function - ROM external low , with Kernal, RAM - Bank 0 and I/O
14	$01 = %00000001	Kernal with BASIC, Character - generator and RAM - Bank 0
15	$00 = %00000000	Kernal with BASIC, I/O and RAM - Bank 0

The command "BANK 15" is the the configuration when the computer is turned on.

CHAPTER 10

AUTOSTART

10.1 AUTOSTART FROM THE DISK DRIVE

Many first time Commodore computer users have difficulty in starting their first program; they have not yet learned "computerese". On some computer systems, MS-DOS computers for example, it is possible to start a program by simply turning the computer on and inserting a disk in the disk drive. To start a program with the CP/M and MS-DOS operating systems all you have to do is type in the name of the program and press the <RETURN> key.

In the C-64 it was a little harder. You had to enter LOAD, the name of the program, "8" (maybe even ",8,1"). But admittedly the C-64 was designed for hobbyist programmers, people with some experience in using computers. The C-128 is aimed at a different group, the business user, and because of this it is equipped with the CP/M operating system. As a result it is possible to load programs automatically from disc, starting them when the computer is first turned on. This "autostart" routine is also called by resetting the computer.

This "autostart" routine holds several possibilities. You can load any number of blocks from disk (but they have to start in sequence from track 1, sector 1) before you load any program. After loading you can execute the program. So you could load in a new language (for example FORTH), then a program in the new language and then switch on the new language. The same can be done with BASIC programs. We'll only know how many possibilities there are after the C-128 is on the market for a while.

In the next section we will explain the autostart routine in detail. If you only want to use the autostart, you don't have to study this section simply use the programs presented here. But if you want to know more about how these procedures operate, you should continue reading.

10.1.1. THE BOOT-CALL ROUTINE

The boot-call routine is located in the operating system from $F890 - $F98A. You should call it with address $FF53; this is where it is located in the kernal jump table.

First the listing of the routine:

```
F890      STA $BF
F892      STX $BA
F894      TXA
F895      JSR $F23D
- - - - - - - - - - - - - -
F898      LDX #$00
F89A      STX $9F
F89C      STX $C2
F89E      INX
F89F      STX $C1
- - - - - - - - - - - - - -
F8A1      INY
F8A2      BNE $F8A1
F8A4      INX
F8A5      BNE $F8A1
- - - - - - - - - - - - - -
F8A7      LDX #$0C
F8A9      LDA $FA08,X
```

```
F8B0      BPL $F8A9
- - - - - - - - - - - - - - -
F8B2      LDA $BF
F8B4      STA $0106
F8B7      LDA #$00
F8B9      LDX #$0F
F8BB      JSR $F73F
F8BE      LDA #$01
F8C0      LDX #$15
F8C2      LDY #$FA
FAC4      JSR $F731
F8C7      LDA #$00
F8C9      LDY #$0F
F8CB      LDX $BA
F8CD      JSR $F738
F8D0      JSR $FFC0
F8D3      BCS $F8EB
- - - - - - - - - - - - - - -
F8D5      LDA #$01
F8D7      LDX #$16
F8D9      LDY #$FA
F8DB      JSR $F731
F8DE      LDA #$0D
F8E0      TAY
F8E1      LDX $BA
F8E3      JSR $F738
F8E6      JSR $FFC0
F8E9      BCC $F8EE
- - - - - - - - - - - - - - -
F8EB      JMP $F98B
- - - - - - - - - - - - - - -
F8EE      LDA #$00
F8F0      LDY #$0B
F8F2      STA $AC
F8F4      STY $AD
- - - - - - - - - - - - - - -
F8F6      JSR $F9D5
- - - - - - - - - - - - - - -
F8F9      LDX #$00
F8FB      LDA $0B00,X
F8FF      CMP $E2C4,X
F901      BNE $F8EB
F903      INX
```

```
F901      BNE  $F8EB
F903      INX
F904      CPX  #$03
F906      BCC  $F8FB
- - - - - - - - - - - - - - - -
F908      JSR  $FA17
F90B      0D 42 4F 4F 54 49 4E
F912      47 20 00
- - - - - - - - - - - - - - - -
F915      LDA  $0B00,X
F918      STA  $A9,X
F91A      INX
F91B      CPX  #$07
F91D      BCC  $F917
- - - - - - - - - - - - - - - -
F91F      LDA  $0B00,X
F922      BEQ  $F92A
F924      JSR  $FFD2
F927      INX
F928      BNE  $F91F
F92A      STX  $9E
- - - - - - - - - - - - - - - -
F92C      JSR  $FA17
F92F      2E 2E 2E 0D
F933      00
- - - - - - - - - - - - - - - -
F934      LDA  $AE
F936      STA  $C6
- - - - - - - - - - - - - - - -
F938      LDA  $AF
F93A      BEQ  $F945
F93C      DEC  $AF
F93E      JSR  $F9B3
F941      INC  $AD
F943      BNE  $F938
F945      JSR  $F98B
- - - - - - - - - - - - - - - -
F948      LDX  $9E
F94A      .BYTE $2C
F945      INC  $9F
F94D      INX
F94E      LDA  0B00,X
F951      BNE  $F94B
```

```
F953      INX
F954      STX $04
- - - - - - - - - - - - - -
F956      LDX $9E
F958      LDA #$3A
F95A      STA #0B00,X
F95D      DEX
F95E      LDA $BF
F960      STA $0B00,X
F963      STX $9E
- - - - - - - - - - - - - -
F965      LDX $9F
F967      BEQ $F97E
F969      INX
F96A      INX
F96B      TXA
F96C      LDX $9E
F96E      LDY #$0B
F970      JSR $F731
F973      LDA #$00
F975      TAX
F976      JSR $F73F
F979      LDA #$00
F97B      JSR $F269
- - - - - - - - - - - - - -
F97E      LDA #$0B
F980      STA $03
F982      LDA #$0F
F984      STA $02
F986      JSR $02CD
- - - - - - - - - - - - - -
F989      CLC
F98A      RTS
```

The first two instructions store the contents of the accumulator and the
X-register in the zero page. The function of these two bytes are: the
accumulator represents the device address of the disk drive, from where
you load a program. The X-register contains the device address of the
disk drive, where you will search the disk for an autostart sequence. In
most cases these bytes are identical. During a reset both register contents

are set to 8. You execute an autostart only on the disk drive with a device address of 8. A programmer can jump to this routine in many different ways, for example, with `SYS DEC ("FF53"),9,9`. This command searches a disk drive with device address 9 for the autostart track and sector.

The subprogram, called in address $F895, closes all files with the device address in the accumulator. The function is clear: the commands and data, which are supposed to be sent to the disk, wouldn't reach the disk quickly enough if a file was still open.

The files close in the following manner: first a table is searched which contains the device address of the present open files for the determined device number. The computer finds the device number in this table ($0362 - $036B) then it finds the respective file number (the information in both tables are in the same place). This file is closed with the kernal routine CLOSE ($FFC3). This happens with all open files (the amount is in $98). There is a third related table at ($0376 - $037F), this contains the secondary addresses of the open files (in the same sequence as the other two tables).

The next five instructions of the boot-call-routine set the following zero page bytes to the following values:

```
$9F   (159):   00
$C1   (193):   01
$C2   (194):   00
```

The address $9F is a counter and will be used later.

In $C1 is the track number, in $C2 is the sector number of the block of the disk where the information to be loaded is located. The information for the "autostart" boot-call is on track 1, sector 0--the first block on the disk. This block may not be used for any other data storage if you wish to make an "autostart" disk. The ideal solution is, to use only "fresh" formatted disks for "autostart" programs. Or check with a disk monitor to see if the block is used or not on disks that contain data.

Track 1 and sector 0 are not only used for the autostart routine, but also to load the CP/M operating system. CP/M uses the autostart routine to load and execute the new operating system. The next four commands (from $F8A1 - $F8A6) are a delay loop. Then 13 bytes from the operating system (from $FA08 - $FA14) are copied into the RAM (from $0100 - $010C). These bytes have the following values:

```
FA08:   30 30 20 31 30 20 30 20 33 31 3A 31 55
```

When you translate these characters to ASCII format and put them in sequence you will receive the following command:

```
U1:   13 0 01 00"
```

If you are familiar with disk drive commands, the command sequence will make sense to you. If you are not familiar with the disk drive commands, please be patient.

The two instructions from \$F8B2 - \$F8B6 store the contents from \$BF to a string. At the start of the routine the address \$BF was loaded with the chosen device address. That means, you write the device address instead of the single zero into the string.

The next eleven instructions have the following function:

Value	Location	Function
#00	\$C6	Bank - Number for LOAD/SAVE/VERIFY
#0F	\$C7	Bank - Number for present file name
#01	\$B7	Length of present Filename
#15	\$BB	Low - byte address of file name
#FA	\$BC	High - byte address of file name
#00	\$B8	Logic data -file number
#0F	\$B9	Secondary address
#BA	\$BA	Device address

So, the file name is in address \$FA15. In this address is the value \$49 (73). This value is the ASCII value of the character "I". Then the instruction following (JSR \$FFC0) calls the kernal routine OPEN. These assembler instructions are the same as the following BASIC command:

```
OPEN 0, Deviceaddress, 15, "I"
```

The "I" stands for the disk command "INITIALIZE". This command reads the BAM (Block Availability Map) of the inserted floppy disk. This command is used to check the disks for different IDs. The ID on the disk tells the drive if a new disk has been inserted since the last time it read the BAM. The Block Availability Map keeps track of the free space on the disk. If you switch disks that have the same ID, the drive still thinks the old disk is inserted; this can can cause a great deal of trouble. The programmers of the C-128 didn't trust that all of your disks would have different IDs, so they inserted this command.

Using the file number zero you can send commands to the disk drive. In address $F8D3 is a BRANCH instruction. This jumps to address $F8EB if the disk drive didn't report its presence on the serial bus (for example, when it is switched off). In this case you don't get an error message. Try it out with the following command (you probably don't have your disk drive switched to device address 10).

```
SYS DEC ("FF53"), 10,10
```

"READY" will appear again.

When the disk drive reports its presence on the serial bus, you continue at address $F8D5. There you set more parameters:

Value	Comes after	Function
#01	$B7	Length of the present file name
#16	$BB	Low - byte address of file name
#FA	$BC	High - byte address of file name
#0D	$B8	Logic data - file number
#0D	$B9	Secondary address
#BA	$BA	Device address

The value $23 (35) is in address $FA16, which is the pointer in $BB/$BC. The filename is "#".

The assembler instructions (with the call of the OPEN Routine in $F8E6) is the same as the following BASIC command:

OPEN 13, Deviceaddress, 13, " # "

In case you are not familiar with the disk drive, this reserves a buffer in the disk drive, for the information to be read from the disk. You have access to this buffer over channel 13.

Here you leave the boot-call routine if the disk is not present in the disk drive.

The four instructions from $F8EE - $F8F5 set the bytes $AC/$AD to $0B00 (the cassette buffer). These two zero page addresses are used as a pointer; the cassette buffer is used to store the characters read from the disk.

Address $F8F6 sends a command to the disk drive and characters are called accordingly. This important routine is listed and documented below:

```
F9D5    LDX   #$00        ; Logic Filenumber
F9D7    JSR   $FFC9       ; Output device with Device
                            address of file number 0
F9DA    LDX   #$0C        ; Amount of Chars to send-1
F9DC    LDA   $0100,X     ; Call Character
F9DF    JSR   $FFD2       ; And Send (BSOUT)
F9E2    DEX               ; All Characters ?
F9E3    BPL   $F9DC       ; No
F9E5    JSR   $FFCC       ; Close Present I/O Channel
                            at IEC - Bus (CLRCH)
F9E8    LDX   #$0D        ; Logic Filenumber
```

```
F9EA    JSR   $FFC6      ; Device address of file
                           with number 13
F9ED    LDY   #$00       ; Counter to zero
F9EF    JSR   $FFCF      ; Enter Character (BASIN)
F9F2    JSR   $F7BC      ; And store in Address
                           determined by $AC/$AD (in
                           bank determined at $C6)
F9F5    INY              ; Raise offset for pointer
                           $AC/$AD
F9F6    BNE   $F9EF      ; Still not all characters
                           (1 Block)
F9F8    JMP   $FFCC      ; Close present I/O Channel
                           at IEC-Bus and Jump back
```

In this case the message "U1:13 0 01 00" is sent and the block at track 1, sector 0 is read into the buffer. This buffer is read and the bytes from $0B00 - $0BFF are stored. Then you continue the boot-call routine.

Next the contents of the addresses $E2C4 - $E2C6 are compared with the first three bytes that were read in. If one of these bytes is different, you leave the routine just as if the disk wasn't present. This means these three bytes contain the information determining whether an autostart will be performed or not! The three bytes in the operating system have the following values:

```
$E2C4 : $43 (67)  "C"
$E2C5 : $42 (66)  "B"
$E2C6 : $4D (77)  "M"
```

The first three bytes from track 1, sector 0 together build the string "CBM".

If all the bytes are equal, the message "(CR) BOOTING" will be output on the screen. This uses the kernal routine PRIMM.

Then the contents of the addresses $0B03 - $0B06 are copied to the addresses $AC - $AF. The contents of the addresses $0B03 - $0B06 equal the bytes 3 - 6 of the block called from disk. We'll explain the function of these bytes later.

In the next section, locations $0B07 to the next zero (0) are interpreted in ASCII and the respective characters are output. The location where the zero appeared is stored in $9E.

Then the PRIMM routine is called again and the text "...(CR)" is output. The next two instructions copy the contents of address $AE to $C6. Additionally, the address $AE was loaded with the contents of $0B05, byte 5 of the block read from the disk. Also, the address $C6 was used before, in a previous routine. There the bank where the block was supposed to be loaded was determined by the content of $C6.

In the next section the content of $AF is called. If it is different than zero one will be subtracted from the value. If it is zero, you jump to another subprogram:

```
F9B3      LDX   $C2        ; Sector Number
F9B5      INX              ; Raise one
F9B6      CPX   #$15       ; Already Sector 21?
F9B8      BCC   $F9BE      ; No
F9BA      LDX   #$00       ; yes, then Sector = 0
F9BC      INC   $C1        ; And Track No. raise one
F9BE      STX   $C2        ; Sector No. store again
F9C0      TXA              ; Sector No. in ACCU
F9C1      JSR   $F9FB      ; Sector No.to ASCII code
```

```
F9C4      STA   $0100     ; Lower Nibble
F9C7      STX   $0101     ; Upper  Nibble
F9CA      LDA   $C1       ; Get Track No.
F9CC      JSR   $F9FB     ; Change to ASCII characters
F9CF      STA   $0103     ; Lower Nibble
F9D2      STA   $0104     ; Upper Nibble
- - - - - - - - - - - - - - - - - - - - - - - - - -
F9D5    - F9FA            ;    Documented above
- - - - - - - - - - - - - - - - - - - - - - - - - -
F9FB      LDX   #$30      ; Upper Nibble = "0"
F9FD      SEC             ; Set carry-flag for subtrac.
F9FE      SBC   #$0A      ; Is number 0-9?
FA00      BCC   $FA05     ; yes, then end
FA02      INX             ; No, then raise number
FA03      BCS   $F9FE     ; And try again
FA05      ADC   #$3A      ; Change low nibble to ASCII
FA07      RTS
```

The subprogram changes numbers to ASCII values; it only functions with
two decimal numbers. Don't forget this when you use the routine for
your own purposes.

So, you may ask, what is the function of the rest of the boot-call routine?

The content from $AF determines how many blocks are to be read from
disk; $AC - $AD determines, which address those blocks are to be stored
(you can't skip pages, the blocks are stored in sequence) and $AE
determines the bank where the blocks are stored. The blocks go in
sequence, track 1, sector 1 then track 1, sector 2 etc.

But there is more. Regardless of if there are more blocks read or not, you
close the opened files in address $F945.

Then you repeat the counter. Which counter? You might remember that in $9E was stored the location where the string ended. Increment this counter and get the character at which the counter shows. If it is zero you leave this section of the boot-call routine. If it is not zero, increment the indicator by one. If zero, increment the indicator again and store it in $04.

In the next section you use the indicator $9E as an offset. At the location of the first zero goes the ASCII value for the colon and before that the content of $BF. The new counter is now stored. Then, the length of the file name is placed into the X-register. If it is zero, you jump over this part, because you know another program is supposed to be called. But, if it is not zero, it is incremented by two, because the colon and the contents of $BF have been added. Then more parameters are set:

Value	Comes After	Function
ACCU	$B7	Length of present file name
$9E	$BB	Low-byte address of file name
#0B	$BC	High-byte address of file name
#00	$CC	Bank-No. for LOAD/SAVE/VERIFY
#00	$C7	BANK-No. for Present file name

In address $F979 the accumulator is loaded with a zero to signal that a LOAD is required. The subprogram, called in the next instruction, is also used by VERIFY. In that case, the flag would be 1.

Then you load the program. You continue at address $F97E, whether a program was loaded or not.

Next in address $0004, the value $0B is stored then in $0002 the value
$0F. Then you jump to the subprogram which is also used by the kernal
routine. This call does the following: you select the bank, with the
number in $0002. Then you jump to the address, determined through
$0003/$0004. This program will be executed. Should this subprogram
be left with a RTS, the program continues in the bank from which you
called the program (in this case address $F989).

In address $F989 you clear the carry-flag. This indicates that the
boot-call routine was left properly (if the disk drive did not report, the
carry-flag would be set, see address $F8D3). The routine is left with a
RTS.

10.1.2. USING THE BOOT - CALL

By examining the boot-call routine in the previous chapter, we found out
that the first block on a disk, track 1/sector 0, must have the following
byte assignment:

    1.   Byte: $43 (67) ASCII-Value for "C"
    2.   Byte: $42 (66) ASCII-Value for "B"
    3.   Byte: $4D (77) ASCII-Value for "M"
    4.   Byte: Low-byte of address, from which more blocks are
         stored (comes in address $AC)
    5.   Byte: High-Byte of this address (comes after $AD)
    6.   Byte: Bank-number, in which the blocks are to be stored
         (comes after $AE)

7.   Byte: Number of blocks to read (comes after $AF)

- -

8.   Byte: To the first zero: Text, given out after BOOTING.
     Behind the first zero to the second: The name of the
     program, which should be loaded after loading the blocks.
     Behind the second zero up to the end program which shall
     be executed after loading.

Let's try out the new knowledge and create an "autostart" disk.:

```
10 OPEN 1,8,15
20 OPEN 2,8,13,"#"
25 PRINT #1,"B-F 0 1 0"
30 PRINT #1,"B-P 13 0"
40 PRINT #2,"CBM"
50 PRINT #1,"U2 13 0 1 0"
60 PRINT #1,"B-A 0 1 0"
70 CLOSE 2
80 CLOSE 1
```

If you are not familiar with disk drive commands here is an explanation of
the program.   First you open a data file, giving you access to the
command channel of the disk drive. Then you reserve a buffer in the disk
drive. This is because data cannot be written directly to the disk, it has to
go in a data buffer. In line 25 a block is marked as free. Important! Any
program on that block will be erased!

In line 30 a pointer is set to the first byte of this buffer. After this, the
character sequence "CBM" is written into this buffer. The instruction in
line 50 will write the data buffer to the disk on the block at track 1, sector
0. In line 60 this block is marked as "used" and the files are closed.

Now call the boot - call routine:

```
SYS DEC ("FF53"),8,8 (or SYS DEC ("F890"),8,8)
```

The disk drive starts and after a short time the text "BOOTING..." will be output on the screen. Then the computer will probably jump into the monitor. Why? Because we assigned the first three bytes of the block, only the bytes that permit the autostart. The rest of the block was probably filled with zeros, so the computer did not get any more text and didn't search for any more blocks or programs. After that the computer tried to execute a machine language program, but found only zeros. These zeros represent the machine language instruction BRK, so it jumped to the monitor (the normal reaction of the C-128 to the BREAK instruction).

Let's enter some more values into our "autostart" program.

```
10 DIM BY (255)
20 BY(0)=ASC("C"): BY(1)=ASC("B"): BY(2)=ASC("M")
30 BY(3)=0: BY(4)=0: BY(5)=0: BY(6)=0
40 PRINT CHR$(147);"TEXT BEHIND 'BOOTING':"
50 FOR ZA=7 TO 252
60 GET KEY A$: IF A$=CHR$(13) THEN 80
70 BY(ZA)=ASC(A$): NEXT ZA
80 BY(ZA)=0
90 ZA=ZA+1: BY(ZA)=0
100 ZA=ZA+1: BY(ZA)=96
110 OPEN 1,8,15
120 OPEN 2,8,13,"#"
125 PRINT #1,"B-F 0 1 0"
130 PRINT #1,"B-P 13 0"
140 FOR ZA=0 TO 255
150 PRINT #2,CHR$(BY(ZA));
160 NEXT ZA
170 PRINT #1,"U2 13 0 1 0"
```

```
180 PRINT #1,"B-A 0 1 0"
190 CLOSE 2
200 CLOSE 1
```

Here you first create an array with 256 elements. The first seven bytes of this array (later written to the autostart block) are set, so that the autostart can be identified without loading any more blocks. Then you can enter any text, but no more than 246 characters. That happens in the following lines:

Line 80:   End of string to output

Line 90:   End of program name

               (0 characters, no program is loaded)

Line 100:   Program to execute (the command: RTS)

Then the bytes are written to disk. Start the boot-call routine again after running this program. Your text is printed and you are returned to BASIC.

Now for a program using the autostart. When you run the following program, the block at track 1, sector 0 will be written so that it starts a (BASIC) program with name "HELLO" automatically. The assignment of the bytes is as follows:

Byte 0- 6   : Bits for autostart routine

Byte 7 - 26 : Text to print out

Byte 27   : Zero as end mark

Byte 28 - 32 : Name of program to load ("HELLO")

Byte 33   : Zero as end mark

Byte 34 - 52 : Machine Program to Execute (RUN)

Now the complete "autostart" program:

```
10 OPEN 1,8,15
20 OPEN 2,8,13,"#"
25 PRINT #1,"B-F 0 1 0"
30 PRINT #1,"B-P 13 0"
40 FOR ZA=0 TO 52
50 READ A
60 PRINT #2,CHR$(A);
70 NEXT ZA
80 PRINT #1,"U2 13 0 1 0"
90 PRINT #1,"B-A 0 1 0"
100 CLOSE 2
110 CLOSE 1
1000 DATA 67,66,77,0,0,0,0
1010 DATA 13,40,67,41,32,49,57,56,53,32,66
1020 DATA 89,32,65,66,65,67,85,83,32
1030 DATA  0
1040 DATA 72,69,76,76,79
1050 DATA  0
1060 DATA 162,2,189,50,11,157,74,3,202,16,247
1070 DATA 169,3,133,208,96,82,213,13
```

The assembler program (data in lines 1060 & 1070) is as follows:

```
         1    LDX #$02           ; Counter
  Loop   2    LDA table,X        ; Get Character
         3    STA $034A,X        ; And in Keyboard Buffer
         4    DEX                ; One more Character?
         5    BPL Loop           ; Yes
         6    LDA #$03           ; Amount of characters
         7    STA $D0            ; In Keyboard Buffer
         8    RTS                ; End of Routine
  Table  9    $52, $D5, $0D      ; ASCII for R,Shift+U
                                 ; And RETURN
```

The machine language routine also stores RUN in the keyboard buffer.

After you have modified your disk with the above program, call the boot-call routine again or reset your computer. The text will be output, but then you receive a "FILE NOT FOUND" message. Of course, this is because the file name "HELLO" is not on the disk. What could a "HELLO" program look like? Like this for example :

```
10  PRINT CHR$(147)
20  PRINT"ENTER CHOICE:"
30  PRINT: PRINT"(1) DIRECTORY"
40  PRINT: PRINT"(2) LOAD PROGRAM"
50  PRINT: PRINT"(3) DISC-OPERATION"
60  PRINT: PRINT: PRINT"(4) FINISH"
70  GET KEY A$: A=VAL(A$)
80  ON A GOTO 100,200,300,400
90  GOTO 70
100 PRINT CHR$(147)
110 DIRECTORY
120 PRINT: PRINT"- PRESS ANY KEY TO CONTINUE-"
130 GET KEY A$: GOTO 10
200 PRINT CHR$(147)
210 INPUT "NAME OF PROGRAM"-,NA$
220 LOAD NA$,8,1
300 PRINT CHR$(147)
310 INPUT "COMMAND"-,BF$
320 OPEN 1,8,15
330 PRINT#1 ,BF$
340 CLOSE 1
350 GOTO 10
400 PRINT CHR$(147)
410 PRINT"ARE YOU SURE (Y/N)?"
420 GET KEY A$: IF A$="N" THEN 10
430 IF A$<>"Y" THEN 420
```

But there are many other possibilities. You could change the name of the program called from the boot-call to automatically load your favorite game or the program you work with most.

The boot-call routine can also load more blocks. You can load a different operating system, a different language, etc, etc..

The respective data has to be in sequence on the disc (starting at track 1, sector 1) and is loaded in the memory in sequence. The bytes that determine this loading are the bytes 3 - 6 on block track 1, sector 0 (see above).

No doubt this routine will be used very often, probably by every commercial program written for the C-128. But you can use it for your own purposes.

10.2. AUTOSTART BY CARTRIDGE

Who hasn't used them, those little boxes called cartridges that are inserted in the expansion port? This automatic start by cartridge has two advantages:

a) It is user friendly; the user doesn't have to enter inconvenient
   SYS commands.
b) The cartridge is harder to copy.

But how does this autostart work? In the C-64 it worked as follows.

When the computer was reset it examined the memory locations $8004 - $8008. If it found the ASCII values of the character sequence "CBM80", it did an indirect jump to the address pointed to in $8000/$8001; which means it called the contents of $8000 as the low byte of the address and the contents of $8001 as the high byte.   Then the computer jumped to this address.

The C-128 works about the same. After a reset, the computer jumps to a subprogram that compares some bytes with fixed values. You will find this routine in memory from $E1F0 - $E241:

```
E1F0    LDX  #$F5
E1F2    LDY  #$FF
E1F4    STX  $C3
E1F6    STY  $C4
E1F8    LDA  #$C3
E1FA    STA  $02AA
E1FD    LDY  #$02
E1FF    LDX  #$7F
E201    JSR  $02A2
E204    CMP  $E2C4,Y
E207    BNE  $E224
E209    DEY
E20A    BPL  $E201
E20C    LDX  #$F8
E20E    LDY  #$FF
E210    STX  $C3
E212    STY  $C4
E214    LDY  #$01
E216    LDX  #$7F
E218    JSR  $02A2
E21B    STA  $0002,Y
E21E    DEY
E21F    BPL  $E218
E221    JMP  ($0002)
- - - - - - - - - - - - - - - -
E224    LDA  #$40
E226    STA  $FF00
E229    LDA  #$24
E22B    LDY  #$E2
E22D    STA  $FFF8
E230    STY  $FFF9
E233    LDX  #$03
E235    LDA  $E2C3,X
```

```
E238    STA  $FFF4,X
E23B    DEX
E23C    BNE  $E235
E23E    STX  $FF00
E241    RTS
```

First the vector at ($C3/$C4) points to address $FFF5. Then it jumps to a routine which calls any address from any bank. Here it calls the contents of address $FFF7 in Bank 1. This byte will be compared with the content of address $E2C6. If these two bytes not identical it jumps to address $E224. If they are equal, it tests the next bytes. The following addresses are compared:

$FFF5 with $E2C4 : $43 (="C")

$FFF6 with $E2C5 : $42 (="B")

$FFF7 with $E2C6 : $4D (="M")

So, unlike the C-64, only three bytes are tested, which are enough. These three bytes equal the string "CBM", which is also used in the autostart routine of the disk drive. If these are identical, you call the contents of the addresses $FFF8 and $FFF9 and store it in the address $0002 and $0003. Over this vector an indirect jump is carried out. To execute an autostart, the following bytes must be assigned as follows:

$FFF5: $43 ("C")

$FFF6: $42 ("B")

$FFF7: $4D ("M")

$FFF8: Low-Byte determined jump - address

$FFF9: High-Byte determined jump - address

The routine jumped to in case of an error must be in Bank 15. Jumping to a routine at $A000 in the RAM of Bank 0 doesn't work, because the BASIC interpreter is in Bank 15. But you can jump to a routine in the cassette buffer, which is shared by the respective memory configuration.

Here is a short explanation before we show some examples of the uses of the cartridge autostart. When the bytes are not equal you don't jump to BASIC as in the C-64.

At address $E224 the first two instructions select the memory configuration for Bank 15. The only difference is that you select RAM Bank 1 instead of RAM Bank 0 (remember: RAM BANK 15 turns on all the system ROMs). Then you store the following values in the addresses $FFF5 - $FFF9:

```
$FFF5:    $43  ("C")
$FFF6:    $42  ("B")
$FFF7:    $4D  ("M")
$FFF8:    $24
$FFF9:    $E2
```

That's why an autostart is performed after every reset, but only with the normal reset routine.

Now take a look at these bytes: enter the monitor and enter M 1FFF5. As you can see, the addresses $FFF5 - $FFF9 are assigned with the values above. Now enter your own address for the autostart: change byte $24 to $4D. Now change byte $E2 to $FF. You now will jump to address $FF4D instead of address $E224 when a reset occurs. This address initializes the C-64 mode. Try it out: push the reset button. After a short time (the 80 column screen might start to blink) you are in the C-64 mode.

And another thing: switch the computer off for a very short time and then back on. As you can see, the computer comes on in the C-64 mode! No, don't be afraid; it is not broken. In the C-128 the RAMs don't clear as fast as in the C-64. That's why the values from $FFF5 - $FFF9 stayed in the computer. Turn your computer off for a little bit longer and you will come back in the C-128 mode. The longer "life" of the RAMs has two advantages: first, a power loss does not affect the operation of the computer; and second, your programs stay in the computer after you switched it off for a short time.

Of course, you can also start BASIC programs with a reset. You have to change the vector at $FFF8 - $FFF9 to your own routine, which simulates the RUN command. In the C-64 it was possible with the following assembler commands:

```
JSR $A659    ;CHRGET On Program start + CLR
JMP $A7AE    :Interpreter loop
```

We can accomplish the same thing on the C-128 in a different manner. Because the C-128 has a keyboard buffer, we store the string RUN and RETURN in the buffer and then quit the program. This starts the BASIC program in memory. An assembler listing would look as follows:

```
        LDX #$02              ;Counter
Loop    LDA table,X          ;GET CHARACTER
        STA $034A,X          ;In the Keyboard Buffer
        DEX                  ;One more Character?
        BPL Loop             ;Yes
        LDA #$03             ;Number of characters
        STA $D0              ;In the Keyboard Buffer
        RTS

Table $52, $D5, $0D          ;ASCII for R,SHIFT+U
                             ;And RETURN
```

CHAPTER 11

C-128 MEMORY

11.1 IMPORTANT ADDRESSES

The C-128's new BASIC is one of the most complete BASICs available on a microcomputer today. But with the C-128 you can do a lot more than the standard BASIC commands allow--without using machine language. The key is the zero page, which is made up of the first 256 memory locations. They contain a lot of pointers and addresses used by the operating system. Modifying these pointers and addresses will let you create your own special operating system, allowing you to do things not possible with normal BASIC commands.

The Commodore 128 has several zero pages, because its operating system is more complex than those used by previous Commodore computers. is more complex than those used by previous Commodore computers.

The following pages contain interesting memory locations and suggestions for using them. Don't be afraid of destroying your computer when modifying the memory locations. About the worst you can do is lock up the computer, but usually a reset will put everything back to normal. If that fails, then you'll have to turn off the computer and turn it back on.

Beside the addresses of the C-128 you will find the corresponding C-64 addresses in parentheses. This means you can translate your old C-64 programs to the new C-128. Both modes are fairly compatible.

Here are some interesting memory locations and their functions.

(decimal location)   (comment)
----
45 - 46   (43-44)   **BASIC Start (Bank O)**

This memory location contains the start address of where the BASIC
programs are stored in the memory (in Low-byte/High-byte formula,
Bank 0). The command:

```
PRINT  PEEK(45)+256*PEEK(46)
```

prints this address. You can also move the start-of-BASIC address.
To do that type:

```
POKE45, lo:POKE 46, hi:POKE (lo+256*hi)-1,0:NEW
```

This command sequence has to be entered in direct mode. `lo` and `hi`
are the Low-byte/High-byte for the new start address. These bytes are
calculated as follows:

```
HI=INT(address/256): LO=address-(256*HI)
```

You erase the program in the memory if you shift the start of BASIC.
Remember that you usually can't shift the start-of-BASIC. This
memory area is reserved for the operating system!

47 - 48 (45-46) **VARIABLE Start (Bank 1)**

These two bytes point to the start of variable-memory (in bank 1).
This pointer can be read or manipulated like the BASIC start (above).

59 - 60 (57-58)   Current BASIC-Line Number

The current BASIC line number is stored in these bytes. Therefore the readout of these addresses makes sense only in the program mode:

```
10 PRINT "This line #";PEEK(59)+256*PEEK(60);
"in use!"
```

65 - 66 (63-64) Current DATA line number

This pointer is interesting if you use the commands READ and DATA in your programs. It contains the line number of the line where you READ the last DATA element; the following program demonstrates this:

```
10 READ A: IF A=-1 THEN END
20 PRINT"THE ELEMENT A IS IN LINE ";
30 PRINT PEEK(65)+256*PEEK(66);"!"
40 GOTO 10
50 DATA 3,6,4,8,4,6,2,
57 DATA 33,6,4,2,4,2,4,
99 REM TEST PROGRAM
167 DATA 3,7,4,9,6,0,0,
190 DATA 5,7,5,-1
```

This address is also useful in finding errors. You find the error with the pointer that gives you the line number where the error occurred. If your program contains a string and your program allows numerical DATA only, the following BASIC program is handy:

```
10  READ A$:IF ASC(A$)<50 OR ASC(A$)>60 THEN1000
20  A=VAL(A$):IF A=-1 THEN END
30  PRINT A,:GOTO 10
40  DATA 4,3,7,54,3,5,2,444
50  DATA 3,5656,a,3,d,4,2,2,2,:REM Error line
60  DATA 4,6,3,5,6,-1
70  :
1000 REM ERROR MESSAGE
1010 PRINT"IN LINE";PEEK(65)+256*PEEK(66);
1020 PRINT"ERROR FOUND. ONLY NUMBERS ";
1030 PRINT"ARE ALLOWED !"
1040 PRINT"CHANGE THIS!":END
```

208 (198) Number of keys pressed

This pointer contains the number of characters you entered with the keyboard.

```
POKE 208,0
```

clears the keyboard buffer.

213 (203) Keyboard reading

The value of the key actually pressed is stored in this address. It has the value 88 if no key is pressed.

```
10 PRINT CHR$(147);
20 PRINT PEEK(213):GOTO 10
```

prints the value of the key pressed.

215 (---) 40/80-column Flag

This address shows you which screen is active. Bit 7 is set in the 80-column-mode, PEEK(215) = 128:

```
10 A=PEEK(215)
```

The following addresses refer to the 40-column and 80-column screens. These memory locations are revised when switching to the other screen. Therefore, you always find the value for the active screen in these locations.

241 (646) Actual character color

There are 16 colors available for characters on the screen. Normally control-characters are used to turn on the colors. But this is impractical and hard to follow in program listings. Often it is easier to use this memory location. It contains the value of the actual character color (0-15) and is very easy to manipulate.

```
10 A=INT(RND(1)*16) :REM Random number 0-15
20 POKE 241, A:Set character
30 PRINT"*";
40 GOTO 10
```

Here is a short summary of the color combinations:

0	: Black	1	: White	2	: Red
3	: Cyan	4	: Violet	5	: Green
6	: Blue	7	: Yellow	8	: Orange
9	: Brown	10	: Light red	11	: Grey 1
12	: Grey 2	13	: Light green	14	: Light blue
15	: Grey 3		(Only for a 40-column screen)		

0	: Black	1	: Grey 2	2	: Blue
3	: Light blue	4	: Green	5	: Light green
6	: Grey 1	7	: Cyan	8	: Red
9	: Light red	10	: Dark violet	11	: Violet
12	: Brown	13	: Yellow	14	: Grey 3
15	: White				(Only for a 80-column screen)

You don't have these colors if you work with a monochrome screen. The colors are transformed into different shades of green, grey, etc. There are only 5 steps of brightness available for all 16 colors. You have to use colors with different brightness if you want to use them on a monochrome screen. Here is the order of brightness:

1. Black
2. Red, Blue, Brown, Grey 1
3. Violet, Orange, Light red, Grey 2, Light blue
4. Cyan, Yellow, Light green, Grey 3
5. White

The 80-column screen has additional features. The bits 4-7 have the following functions:

    Bit 4 : Flashing
    Bit 5 : Underline
    Bit 6 : Reverse
    Bit 7 : 2nd set of characters

Bits 4 and 5 only affect the next PRINT statement after the POKE command.

```
POKE 241, 15+2^4 : PRINT "TEST"
```

Puts a white, flashing "TEST" on the screen.

```
POKE 241, 2+2^5+2^7 : PRINT "HELLO"
```

The above prints a blue-underlined "HELLO". This means you can mix the different functions! The functions "reverse" (bit 6) and "2nd set of characters" (bit 7) are constant functions; they refer to all following PRINT orders and to the direct mode. A RVS-mode like this cannot be turned off by CRTL+9!

243 (199) RVS-Flag

Corresponding to address 241, this address determines the kind of characters that are to be shown on the screen. Reverse or normal (there is also a control-character for this). 0 = normal, 1 = reverse:

```
10 POKE 243,0:PRINT "NORMAL and.....";
20 POKE 243,1:PRINT ".....REVERSE!"
```


244 (212) Quote-Mode-Flag

Quote-mode means control-characters are not active between quotation marks, but instead display control characters on the screen. If you turn the quote-mode on (=1) the following control characters in a PRINT statement are ignored and their control characters are printed on the screen.

```
POKE 244, 1 : PRINT"{3crsrdwns}{rvson}HELLO !"
```

247 (657) C=/SHIFT Stop-Flag, CRTL-S

You know how to change the character set by pressing the <SHIFT> key and the Commodore key (<C=>). You can also do this while a program is being executed. It doesn't disturb the running program, only what you see on the screen. This can be disabled:

```
POKE 247,128    (locked)
POKE 247,0      (normal)
POKE 247,64     (disable CTRL-S)
```

248 (---) Scrolling Stop-Flag

Once you have reached the lowest screen-line and print on the next line, the screen contents are shifted one row up. You can eliminate this effect:

```
POKE 248, 128 (Scrolling off)
POKE 248, 0     (Normal)
```

249 (---) Beep-Tone Stop-Flag

Here it is possible to disable the beep-tone. It is generated by:

```
PRINT CHR$(7)    (Program-mode)    or
CTRL+G           (Direct-mode)
```

Try this:

```
POKE 249, 128    (off)
POKE 249, 0      (Enables the beep-tone again)
```

By the way: SYS 51602 generates the tone. But you can do more
with the tone than just give a signal.

```
X=100: FOR I=0 TO X:SYS 51602:NEXT I
```

This gives you a longer tone, depending on the X-value.

All the following addresses are common and not tied to the active screen.
They are not in the true zero page.

842-852   (631-640) Keyboard-Buffer

These ten bytes are the buffer for keys entered from the keyboard.
They can be used for many programming applications. There are too
many possibilities to describe here, but we'll give you one example:

```
10 POKE 842, ASC("L"): POKE 843,ASC("I")+128
20 POKE 844,13
30 POKE 208, 3
40 END
```

1024-2023 (1024-2023) 40-Column Screen Memory

These 1000 bytes contain the 40-column screen. This area is not used
if you work with a 80-column screen; you can use it for your own
machine language programs. Otherwise:

```
POKE 1024 +X + 40 * Y,Z

X=Column
Y=Row
Z=Character-code
```

places a character on the 40-column screen.

2592 (649) Maximum Length of the Keyboard-Buffer

The length of the keyboard-buffer is defined with this address.

```
POKE  2592,0     (turns off the buffer, keys are no longer stored)
POKE  2592,10    (normal)
```

The length of the keyboard-buffer should not exceed the maximum 10
because this is the maximum of available space reserved in memory!

2593 (---) CTRL-S Flag

A running program stops when <CTRL-S> is pressed, and continues
when any other key is pressed. Many larger computers have this
function. It is very useful if you only want to interrupt the program

for a short while to have a closer look (or have a quick breakfast). But you can use this address in a completely different way. You simulate the <CTRL-S>. The program stops and waits for the next key pressed.

```
10 PRINT "PRESS ANY KEY "
20 POKE 2593,1
30 PRINT "OK"
```

2594 (650) REPEAT-Flag

The C-128 has a REPEAT-function for all keys. This means if you depress a key for a short period of time the character will be printed continuously.

```
POKE 2594, 0        (space bar and cursor keys)
POKE 2594,64        (no keys with repeat function)
POKE 2594,128       (normal)
```

2595 (651) REPEAT-delay

The computer continues normal printing after a short delay. The delay time can be adjusted with this address, so you can choose a long delay. No delay makes sense as a controller (with a GET).

```
POKE 2595,X
X=delay time
```

2598 (---) VIC Cursor-Mode

This address controls the flash of the cursor, but only the cursor
controlled by VIC chip. This means the address will work only in
40-column mode.

```
Bit 6 : 1=solid
        0=flash
```

```
POKE  2598,0      (Cursor flashes, normal)
POKE  2598,64     (Cursor doesn't flash)
```

2599 (204) VIC Cursor on/off-Flag

This address works only with the 40-column screen. You can activate
the cursor with this address. The following demonstrates what you
can do with this address:

```
Bit 0 : 1=Cursor on
        0=Cursor flash
```

```
10 POKE 2599, 0:REM CURSOR ON
20 PRINT  "HELLO!";
30 FOR  T=1 TO 5000:  NEXT T
40 PRINT  "THAT'S IT!"
50 END
```

This can be used effectively with the command GETKEY. This
command waits for a key press and then stores the character. It is
different from the INPUT command in that the cursor does not flash
to get the user's attention. Here is an example:

```
10   POKE 2599, 0
20   GETKEY A$
30   (. . . )
```

This works with the GET command too.

2603 (---) VDC Cursor-Mode

You can influence the cursor of the 80-column screen at address 2598. The bits of this address mean:

```
Bit 0     1=solid
Bit 2-3   Display in pixel rows
Bit 4-5   Cursor off
Bit 6     1=flash
```

```
POKE 2603, 2^0+2^1+2^2
```

This activates the underline cursor. The thickness of the cursor depends on the bits 2 and 3.

2604 (---) VIC Pointer to Screen-RAM / character set

The content of this address are transferred automatically to address 53272 of the VIC. The contents determine the start addresses of the screen-RAMs and the character generator.

2606 (648) VDC High-Byte of the screen RAMs

This address is responsible for the 80-column screen again. Here you can shift the screen-memory with the registers 12 and 13 of the VDC.

2607 (--) VDC High-Byte of the color memory (attribute-RAM)

The High-Byte of the 80-column attribute-RAM is stored here. It is related to the previous address because you can move the color-memory in the 80-column mode.

2619 (648) VIC Hi-Byte of the screen RAMs

This address has the same function as the address 2606 at the VDC. You find the start address of the 40-column screen-RAM here.

2816-3327 (828-1029)   Cassette buffer

This relatively large area is used by the system only if you work with the Datasette. This area is not used if you use the disk drive. It offers room for machine language routines.

4096-4105 (---) Assignment-length of the function keys

Each of these ten bytes is reserved for one of the ten function keys (<F1-8>, <HELP> and <SHIFT+RUN/STOP>). The length of the function key assignment is stored in these bytes. Set the corresponding byte to zero if you want to turn off the assignment of a function key (for example: if you want to read a key in your own program).

```
POKE 4096,0    (erases assignment of F1)
```

4624-4625 (55-56) Pointer pointing to end-of-BASIC

The highest address of a BASIC program is stored in these bytes (in bank 0):

```
PRINT PEEK (4624)+256*PEEK(4625)
```

The size of your program is easily determined:

```
PRINT (PEEK(4624)+256*PEEK(4625))-
(PEEK(45)+256*PEEK(46))
```

In case you want to write your own machine language program at the end of the memory in bank 0 (BASIC-memory) you can limit the BASIC-memory with these two addresses so that your machine language program is protected from being overwritten.

11.2. JUMP TABLE

Important to every machine language programmer is a solid understanding of the operating system. This allows him/her to create shorter programs in the least amount of time. He/she simply takes prepared routines, instead of writing them. We don't want to write a second *Commodore-128 Internals*, but we'll choose some popular routines and show you how to use them.

There are several jump commands with powerful routines included in both the BASIC interpreter and the operating systems of the C-128 . Let's go to the most important and best-known routines first:

11.2.1 KERNAL

The C-128, like every other Commodore computer, has a Kernal jump table at the end of the ROM. It provides easy access to important kernal routines and allows quick program conversions to other Commodore computers. This table is greatly extended compared to the C-64 or VIC-20. We want to introduce the section of the table from $FF4D-$FF7F.

There are some routines designed exclusively for the C-128. There is, for example, the C-64-mode routine that turns the C-128 into a C-64. There are also some routines to read different memory banks.

Another interesting aspect is that Commodore has assigned a byte with the value zero between the old and new kernal table ($FF80). This is the number of the Kernal table. There is also a new address directly in front of the addresses for NMI, Reset and the IRQ. This address, at $FFF8/$FFF9, points to address $E224 and is called C-128 mode. Let's examine the secrets of the new jump table.

Kernal-address:	$FF4D (65357)
Name:	C64MODE
Real jump-address:	$E24B (57931)
Function:	Transforms the C-128 into the C-64

The name of this function is self-explanatory.

Kernal address:	$FF50 (65360)
Name:	DMA-CALL
Real jump address:	$F7A5 (63397)
Function:	access to the DMA-controller

You can control the DMA-controller (Direct Memory Access) with this routine. This routine becomes interesting with versions of the C-128 with more than 128K RAM, because it works only with the extended RAM.

Kernal-address: $FF53 (65363)
Name: BOOT-CALL
Real jump-address: $F890 (63632)
Function: Load and start program from disk

With this routine you can load and start a program immediately from the disk. It is possible to start programs after turning on the computer, because this routine is called with a reset.

Kernal-address: $FF56 (65366)
Name: PHOENIX
Real jump-address: F867 (63591)
Function: Start external-ROM's

You can start external ROM's (cartridges) with this routine. Immediately after PHOENIX is done, it jumps to the BOOT-CALL routine. This routine is also called with a reset.

Kernal-address: $FF59 (65369)
Name: LKUPLA
Real jump-address: $F79D (63389)
Function: Gets entry for file number

If you call this routine you enter the file number in the accumulator and you get back:

Accumulator: File number
X-Register: Device address
Y-Register: Secondary address

It returns with a set Carry-Flag if the file number was not found. Otherwise this Flag is reset. This routine uses a different routine at $F202. This routine looks to see if a given file number already exists in the X-Register. It returns with a reset Zero-Flag if the file number already exists. Otherwise the Zero-Flag is set.

Kernal-address:	$FF5C (65372)
Name:	LKUPSA
Real jump-address:	$F786 (63366)
Function:	Look up secondary-address

This function is comparable to the last one. But the secondary-address is in the Y-Register. This routine does not look for several equal files with the same secondary-address. It looks up the entry of the first found file belonging to the secondary-address. After the return, all three registers contain the same values as the routine before:

Accumulator:	File number
X-Register :	Device address
Y-Register :	Secondary address

The flags are set the same way.

Kernal address: $FF5F (65375)

Name: SWAPPER

Real jump-address: $C02A (49194)

Function: Switch between 80 / 40 column-screen

The screen is switched if you execute this routine. If you were in the 40 column mode and this routine is called, your input now appears on the 80-column-screen. We will now have a closer look at this routine. Beginning with address $FF5F it jumps to address $CD2E (why make it easy if you can make it complicated?) At $CD2E the following is executed:

```
CD2E      LDX  #$1A
CD30      LDY  $0A40,X
CD33      LDA  $E0,X
CD35      STA  $0A40,X
CD38      TYA
CD39      STA  $E0,X
CD3B      DEX
CD3C      BPL  $CD30
CD3E      LDX  #$0D
CD40      LDY  $0A60,X
CD43      LDA  $0354,X
CD46      STA  $0A60,X
CD49      TYA
CD4A      STA  $0354,X
CD4D      DEX
CD4E      BPL  $CD40
CD50      LDA  $D7
CD52      EOR  #$80
CD54      STA  $D7
CD56      RTS
```

In the first section (up to $CD3D) the memory-blocks $E0-$FA and $0A40-$0A5A are exchanged. In locations $0A40 to $0A5A are stored the screen-values for the screen not currently being used (cursor position, insert-mode-flag, quote-mode-flag, etc.). The routine continues in the same manner when you leave the current screen to switch back to the other screen. Try it out. Get in the quote-mode by entering a quotation mark. Press the cursor keys a few times. Now enter ESC+X (press slowly, one after the other) and enter something on the other screen. Now change back to the other screen and press the cursor keys a few times. As you can see, you are still in the quote-mode. Change to the other screen and enter:

```
POKE DEC("0A54"),0
```

Go back to other screen and press a cursor key; no control-character is printed, but the cursor moves. Why? Because the above POKE sets the quote-mode-flag to zero. This register was copied when you switched back to the other screen and the quote-mode was gone. Therefore, you can predetermine with POKEs how your other screen will look after you switch back. Also, have a look at the addresses in the description of the zero page ($E0-$FA). We'll give you a formula to calculate an address on the closed screen in relation to the one in use:

```
new address=old address +4200  (fantastic isn't it ?)
```

Let's go back to the SWAPPER routine. The next eight commands exchange two more blocks.

a) $0354 - $035E (Tab -Stops) with $0A60-$0A6A
b) $035F - $0361 (Line-links) with $0A6B-$A6D

Between the addresses $CD50-$CD55 the screen is changed. Therefore bit 2 of $D7 is inverted and this ends the routine.

Kernal-address:	$FF62 (65378)
Name:	DLCHR
Real jump-address:	$CO27 (49191)
Function:	Initialize the VDC character-generator

This routine copies the VDC's character-generators for 40 column to that for a 80 column. The character-generator of the VDC doubles its size (to 8K) because it copies eight zero-bytes between each character.

The next seven routines are the most important routines for accessing different banks.

Kernal-address:	$FF68 (65384)
Name:	SETBAK
Real jump-address:	$F73F (63295)
Function:	Verify the bank for SAVE / LOAD / VERIFY

This routine has only 3 commands:

```
$F73F   STA   $C6   ;   bank number, where the program is located.
$F741   STX   $C7   ;   bank number, where the file name is located.
$F743         RTS
```

Vector $BB / $BC contain the address of the file names.

Kernal-address:	$FF6B (65387)
Name:	GETCFG
Real jump-address:	$F7EC (63468)
Function:	Get configuration number.

You have to load the X-register with the number of the desired bank (0-15) before you jump to this routine. You get back a byte in the accumulator. This byte corresponds to the assignment of the MMU's configuration register, so that the desired bank can be chosen. You only have to store it in the address $D500 ($FF00). The chapter about the MMU tells you which memory configurations follow the single bank numbers.

Kernal-address:	$FF6E (65390)
Name:	JSRFAR
Real jump-address:	$02CD (717)
Function:	Starting a subprogram in any bank

This function lets you call a subprogram in any bank. The computer returns to the bank that originally called the routine after it finishes the subprogram. Before calling (you must use JSR) you have to load the following memory locations and registers with the corresponding contents:

$0002:	Number of the desired bank
$0003:	High-byte of the desired address
$0004:	Low-byte of the desired address
$0005:	Desired status-register (to turn off the IRQ, turning on the decimal -modes, etc.)

$0006:	Desired accu
$0007:	Desired X-register
$0008:	Desired Y-register
$0009:	Number of the calling bank

The following addresses contain the new register contents after the return:

$0005:	Status
$0006:	Accu
$0007:	X-register
$0008:	Y-register
$0009:	Stack-pointer

What you do with these values is up to you. You also can load the memory location $0006 into the X-register and save a transfer-command.

Kernal-address:	$FF71 (65393)
Name:	JMPFAR
Real jump-address:	$02E3 (739)
Function:	Jump to a bank

With this routine a jump to any bank is executed. This routine is also used by JSRFAR. Therefore the call is very similar:

$0002:	Number of the desired bank
$0003:	High-byte of the desired address
$0004:	Low-byte of the desired address

$0005:   Desired status-register

$0006:   Desired accu

$0007:   Desired X-register

$0008:   Desired Y-register

Here the call has to be made with the JMP command.

Kernal-address: $FF74 (65369)

Name: INDFET

Real jump-address: $F7D0 (63440)

Function: Get a byte from any bank

With this routine you can get the contents of any bank. Call the routine as follows:

$02B9: Low-byte of the vector pointing to the desired memory location.The vector has to be initialized (it has to contain the desired address split in Low-and High-byte). This vector must be in the zero page.

Accu: Byte, where you want to enter the desired address

X-Reg: Number of the desired bank

Y-Reg: Offset that is eventually added to the address (normally zero, if you don't ask for an index).

Kernal-address:	$FF77 (65399)
Name:	INDSTA
Real address jump:	$F7DA (63450)
Function:	Stores a byte in any bank

This is the opposite of INDFET. To store a byte the following addresses and registers have to be set:

Accu:	Low-byte of the vector
	(it points to the desired address like INDFET).
X-Reg:	Number of the desired bank
Y-Reg:	Offset

Kernal-address:	$FF7A (65402)
Name:	INDCMP
Real jump-address:	$F7E3 (63459)
Function:	Compare accumulator and byte in any bank

This function compares the contents of an address with the contents of the accumulator in any desired bank. The usual flags for comparing are set (Zero-Flag=1 if both are equal, etc.) The following memory locations have to be set before calling:

$02C8:	Vector low-byte pointing to the desired address
Accu:	Character to be compared with the contents of the addressed memory location.
X-Reg:	Number of the desired bank

Kernal-address:	$FF7D (65405)
Name:	PRIMM
Real jump-address:	$FA17 (64023)
Function:	Print a string

The old part of the Kernal contains a routine to print out a single character (BSOUT). You can print out a string with this routine in a simple but clever way. The characters to be printed are simply placed behind the call to the routine. This results in the following:

```
JSR     $FF7D
(any text, a zero for an end mark.)
RTS
```

But how can this be? How does the computer reach the finishing RTS? Let's have a look at the routine again:

```
FA17          PHA
FA18          TXA
FA19          PHA
FA1A          TYA
FA1B          PHA
FA1C          LDY #$00
FA1E          TSX
FA1F          INC $0104,X
FA22          BNE $FA27
FA24          INC $0105,X
FA27          LDA $0104,X
FA2A          STA $CE
FA2C          LDA $0105,X
FA2F          STA $CF
FA31          LDA ($CE),Y
FA33          BEQ $FA3A
FA35          JSR $FFD2
FA38          BCC $FA1F
```

```
FA3A        PLA
FA3B        TAY
FA3C        PLA
FA3D        TAX
FA3E        PLA
FA3F        RTS
```

First the contents of the accumulator and the X-Registers are stored in the stack, then the Y-Register, which is later used with indirect indexed address, as an offset, is stored in the X-Register.

Now the important part of the routine begins. The stack pointer points to the next free location on the stack. To understand what happens you have to know how the stack is built as well as its position. In the C-128 it is located in memory from $0139 to $01FF. The stack pointer first points to $01FF and becomes smaller as more elements are put on the stack.

We'll simulate how the stack reacts when you call it with this routine. Let's say the stack pointer contains the value $F0 and as a result points to the address $01F0. The stack looks something like the picture on the next page:

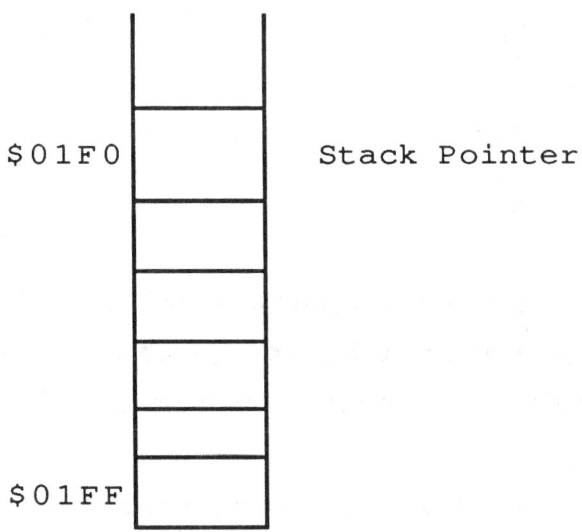

Now the routine is started. First one number is placed on the stack, for the hi-byte of address $2000. The program counter (this register has the pointer, and the next byte of the word) places the next word on the stack, first the hi-byte then the low byte. This results in the following picture:

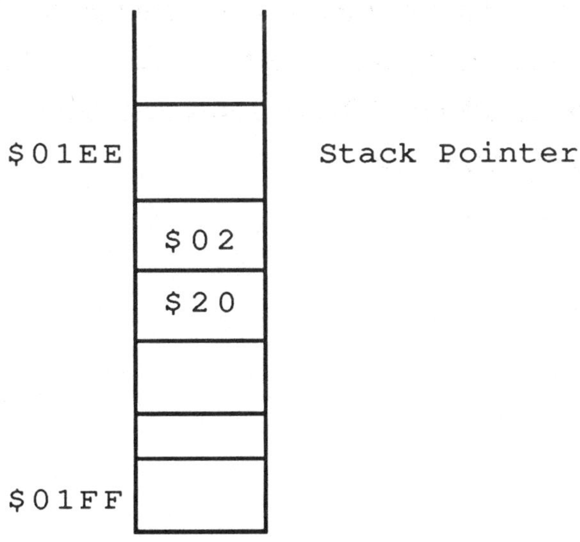

Then the routine fills the next three memory registers and the stack
looks like this:

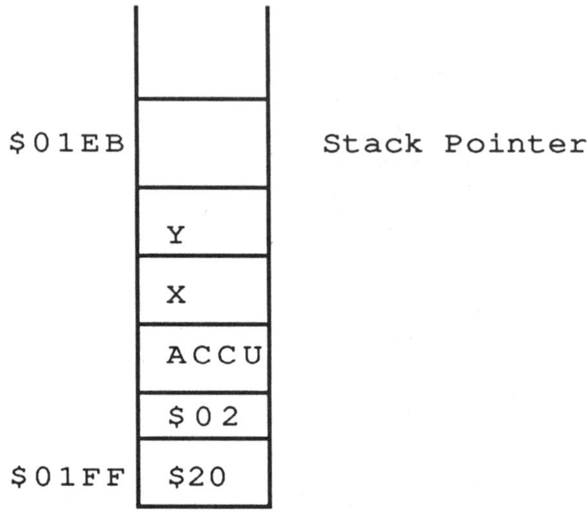

At address $FA1F one byte of the stack is pointed to. But which one?
Let's calculate it. The stack pointer (and therefore the X-register)
contain the value $EB. When you add $0104 you get $01EF. The
low-byte of the return address is raised by one. The BRANCH
command checks if the low-byte is zero. In this case, the byte at
address $0105 + $EB=$01F0, (which is the high-byte of the return
address) is raised by one. The following four commands set the
vector $CE / $CF to the first byte of the string to print.

Now a character is read, checked for zero and printed out if it is not a
zero. With the following BRANCH command all characters are
printed. The register-contents are carried back when the loop is
finished. The result is depicted on the next page:

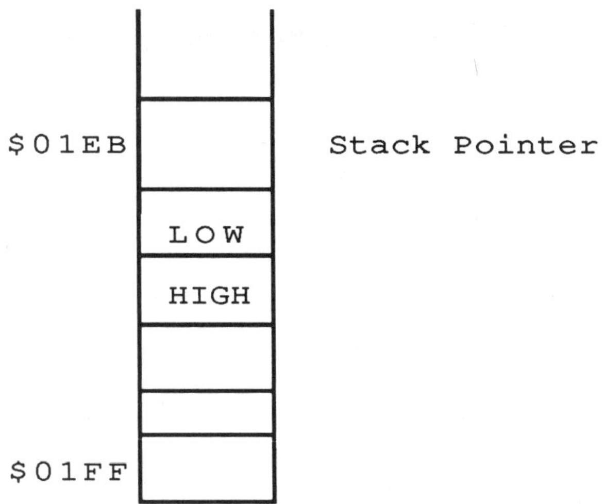

Finally the processor reaches the RTS command and gets the return address from the stack. This address is incremented with every character read so that now it points to the last byte of the string, the end mark zero. Now the processor increments the program-counter and continues on.

The programmers had some good ideas, as you can see. The routine has important advantages. It doesn't require you to load the registers with pointers to the desired string, as is normal. This makes the program shorter, faster and use less memory. Increasing the speed and reducing the memory requirements is always the goal of a good systems programmer.

Those were the Kernal routines. We'll continue with the next section.

11.2.2. VECTOR-LOAD-TABLE

There is a table from $42CE-$4309 in the BASIC-interpreter with which you can easily get memory-locations, defined by vectors. You use these routines as follows: You enter the desired address into the vector and then call the routine belonging to the vector. But this index has some disadvantages:

a) You cannot use every vector, those you can use are listed in the index below.

b) You can not get a byte from any bank.

c) It is not always returned to the original bank.

Look at the index below to see if you can get a byte from a certain bank and return to the same bank! If not you must use the kernal-routine INDFET ($FF74).

Address	Vector	Byte-of	After the return
$42CE	$50/$51	Bank 1	Bank 14 (RAM-Bank 1)
$42D3	$3F/$40	Bank 1	Bank 14 (RAM-Bank1)
$42D8	$52/$53	Bank 1	Bank 14 (RAM-Bank 1)
$42DD	$5C/$5D	Bank 0	Bank 14
$42E2	$5C/$5D	Bank 1	Bank 14 (RAM-Bank 1)
$42E7	$66/$67	Bank 1	Bank 14 (RAM-Bank 1)
$42EC	$61/$62	Bank 0	Bank 14
$42F1	$70/$71	Bank 0	Bank 14
$42F6	$70/$71	Bank 1	Bank 14 (RAM-Bank 1)
$42FB	$50/$51	Bank 1	Bank 14 (RAM-Bank 1)
$4300	$61/$62	Bank 1	Bank 14 (RAM-Bank 1)
$4305	$24/$25	Bank 0	Bank 14

"Bank 14 (RAM-Bank 1)" means: The memory shows the configuration as bank 14 after the switch is over. But RAM-bank 1 is turned on instead of

RAM-bank 0. These routines switch RAM and ROM only; the contents of the ROM-bank are never changed.

11.2.3   KERNAL CALLS

This index is found in the BASIC-interpreter also. Some kernal routines are called here, but Bank 15 is turned on first (the one exception is $928D; it turns on Bank 14).

	Address	Kernal-Routine
	$9251	Get status ($FFB7)
	$9257	Set ($FFBA)
	$925D	Set filename parameter ($FFBD)
	$9263	BASIN ($FFCF)
	$9269	BSOUT ($FFD2)
	$926F	CLRCH ($FFCC)
	$9275	CLOSE ($FFC3)
	$927B	CLALL ($FFE7)
	$9281	PRIMM ($FFE7)
	$9287	SETBNK ($FF68)
	$928D	set/get ($FFF0)
	$9293	Requests stop-key ($FFE1)

11.3. FREE MEMORY

When using machine language programs you have to store them so they are not destroyed by BASIC or the operating system. The BASIC-RAM can be used only if you don't want to enter a BASIC program in the memory (or you set the start-of-BASIC higher, or the end-of-BASIC lower). It is important to know which addresses you can use in zero page. Some addressing modes are only available with pointers in the zero page. These free areas will be shown here. Let's first talk about the zero page.

11.3.1 FREE ZERO PAGE MEMORY

The addresses $FA-$FE in the zero page are always available, as well as the addresses $4E/$4F. These latter two addresses are used only by the boot-call routine (see chapter 10.1).

These are all the free addresses in the zero page. But six addresses are better than none. Other pages used by the operating-system also have free addresses. But using them really makes no sense because you also can use every other address in the memory.

11.3.2   USABLE MEMORY FOR MACHINE LANGUAGE

The C-64 often used two memory locations: the cassette buffer for short programs and the area $C000-$CFFF. A machine language program was usually not placed at the end-of-BASIC or even at the start of BASIC. The C-128 has more possibilities. First there is the cassette buffer, from $0B00-$0BFF. Directly behind the tape buffer are the two buffers for the RS232 interface:

  1. $0C00 - $0CFF = RS232 input buffer
  2. $0D00 - $0DFF = RS232 output buffer

This area is used by very few C-128 users. It offers 768 bytes of storage for machine language programs ($0B00 - $0DFF).

But that's not all. Under normal circumstances the area from $1300 to $1BFF is available. This is nine pages or 2304 bytes of RAM! This area was originally meant for ROM-cartridges.

There is another possibility: put your programs in the RAM-bank 1. This is meant for variables only. You no doubt realize that 64K for variables is a little much; you can use some of this for machine language programs.

The next chapter will show you how to make use of this memory. The C-128 offers many possibilities to arrange your programs in the memory. It is also useful to know that you can do graphics without using your RAM, because the VDC has its own 16K of RAM-memory.

CHAPTER 12

CHANGING THE OPERATING SYSTEM

Because the C-128 is also a C-64, there are routines to switch it into the C-64 mode. BASIC 7.0 has the command GO 64. The new kernal jump table has a routine called "C64 MODE". Let's have a closer look at this routine.

```
E24B      LDA #$E3
E24D      STA $01
E24F      LDA #$2F
E251      STA $00
E253      LDX #$08
E255      LDA $E262,X
E258      STA $01,X
E25A      DEX
E25B      BNE $E255
E25D      STX $D030
E260      JMP $0002
- - - - - - - - - - - - - - - - - - - - - - - - - - -
E263      LDA #$F7
E265      STA $D505
E268      JMP ($FFFC)
```

The first four commands switch the processor-port. The next five commands are a loop. First the addresses $E263 - $E26A to $0002 - $0009 are copied. The command in address $E25D changes the clock speed to 1 MHz. Therefore zero is stored in register 48 of the new VIC (the X-register was set to zero by the loop before). Row by row, the commands copied by the loop are executed. The switching is now made with the first two commands. The memory-location $D505 belongs to the MMU and has the following significance.

Bit-number	:	Function at 0	:	Function at 1
0	:	Z-80	:	6502 on
1 & 2	:	not used now		--
3	:	FSDIR control bit (for disk)		
4	:	C-64	:	C-128
5	:	C-64	:	C-128
6	:	C-128	:	C-64
7	:	40-column	:	80-column

Bits 3 and 4 are read only. The mode is not changed by writing to these bits. These bits represent only the polarity of two pins at the expansion port:

Bit 4 : GAME
Bit 5 : EXROM

These pins are checked every reset. If one of them returns a logic zero, then the C-64 mode is activated. Therefore the C-64 mode is activated immediately if the C-64 cartridges are connected. You also can build a special push button to activate the C-64 mode when desired.

Bit 7 is also read only. This bit gives you the status of the <40/80-DISPLAY> key. When this key is depressed, this bit will be 1. This bit does not show you the actual mode; it is not altered if you change the mode with <ESC+X>. The most important bit is bit 6. The C-128 goes into the C-64 mode if this bit is set (1). Now we can understand the two commands in the C-64 mode routine. The hexadecimal value $F7 is binary 11110111. Bit 6 is set.

The last command finally does the reset. After the switching, before the reset, all ROMs of the C-128 are turned off and those of the C-64 are turned on. If the last three commands were not in RAM Bank 0, but in either ROM or RAM Bank 1, the computer would lock up. Try it, jump to the routine at $E263. The commands are in the RAM and the processor (now a 6510) continues at address $0007 and does a reset (the program counter stayed as it was, of course).

We want to make sure that the RAM Bank 0 is really used by both processors. Let's enter the following:

```
POKE 8192 , 170 : POKE 8193 , 85
GO 64   {and then Y for Yes, of course}
PRINT PEEK(8192);PEEK(8193)
```

You get back the values entered on the screen! If the memory is not erased, then you should be able to transfer complete programs to the C-64! Indeed this works. Try entering a small program, and changing the mode with the command GO 64. Now enter the following POKE's:

```
POKE 43, 1: POKE 44, 28
```

Your program appears back on the screen. You can even execute it. However, commands that the C-64 cannot execute are not allowed in these programs.

It is even possible to continue a program started in the C-128 mode in the C-64 mode without a break. It's necessary to do the largest part of the reset-routine first. Otherwise a lot would go wrong: the IRQ-Vector is not defined, the screens would not be set to normal values, etc...

An example:

```
2000    A9 F7       LDA     #$F7      ; Switch
2002    8D 05 D5    STA     $D505     ; to 64-mode
2005    A2 FF       LDX     #$FF      ; Reset-routine
2007    78          SEI               ; Up to jump
2008    9A          TXS               ; To BASIC-cold start
2009    D8          CLD               ; and test at ROM in
200A    8E 16 D0    STX     $D016     ; $8000
200D    20 A3 FD    JSR     $FDA3
2010    20 50 FD    JSR     $FD50
2013    20 15 FD    JSR     $FD15
2016    20 5B FF    JSR     $FF5B
2019    58          CLI
201A    EE 20 D0    INC     $D020     ; Raise bkgnd color
201d    4C 1A 20    JMP     $1A20     ; once again
```

Now call the routine with the command SYS DEC ("2000"). After a
moment you get a colorful screen--in the C-64 mode.

None of this is easy with BASIC programs. Try it once!

CHAPTER 13

THE C-64 MODE ON THE COMMODORE 128

One real advantage of the C-128 is its compatibility with the C-64. When you switch to the C-64-mode, you're able to use any and all software available for the C-64.

The Commodore people had to take care that all C-64 programs could really be run on the C-128 in the C-64-mode. Therefore they switched the complete system configuration of the C-128 to the C-64. The C-64-mode offers you only the normal BASIC V2.0., thus eliminating the bank switching and the Z-80 processor features. But some features of the C-128 can still be used in C-64 mode.

13.1   HIGH-SPEED ON THE C-64

The C-128 has a video controller, VIC 8564, for the 40-column screen. The Commodore 64 had a VIC 6564. The new VIC is upward compatible to the C-64's VIC 6564. This means it accomplishes the same tasks as the old 6564. There are two new registers added and these registers can also be modified in the C-64 mode! Register 48 plays a special role.

13.1.1   Register 48: Processor-clock

As with the C-64, the 128's clock controls the entire computer. With register 48 you can double the speed of the C-128 from 1 MHz to 2 MHz.

The great thing is that you can double the speed in C-64 mode as well.

This means that all of your "old" C-64 programs can run twice as fast. It also speeds up time consuming routines like the garbage collection. But there is one catch: The VIC uses clock gaps in the system to get a character out of the video RAM to refresh the screen. With the doubled clock speed these gaps are only half size, too short a time for the VIC to refresh the screen. You'll get a lot of strange things on the screen, instead of the normal display. Therefore, you should use the double clock only if the screen content does not matter to you. The routine is done like this:

```
POKE 53296,1    (2    MHz, fast)
POKE 53296,0    (1    MHz, normal)
```

To see what this looks like, enter the following program:

```
10    TI$="000000"
20    :
30    FOR X=1 TO 10000
40    NEXT X
50    :
60    PRINT TI$
```

This program needs 14 seconds to complete the loop. It works faster with the following lines added:

```
20 POKE 53296 , 1 :    REM FAST
50 POKE 53296 , 0 :    REM NORMAL
```

The same loop now takes only 7 seconds!

13.2 80-COLUMN CONTROLLER ACCESS

Yes, you now can access the 80-column controller in the C-64 mode. Finally, a full 80 characters per line. The operating system of the C-64 is not prepared for this controller, but it should not be a problem to copy these routines out of the C-128.

Any examples of this would be beyond the scope of this book. But here are a few suggestions. How about a graphic extension to get access to the 80-character screen in the '64 mode? Or an operating system expansion (in the IRQ) that will be able to write on the 80-character-screen?

13.3   NUMERIC KEYPAD ON THE C-64

This is more of a suggestion than a tip. We'll activate the numeric keypad with a single POKE command in the C-64 mode. Unfortunately, you'll see that the characters don't fit the keys. We didn't have enough time to figure this out before press time. Maybe *you* can activate the numeric keypad completely!

Here's the POKE:

```
POKE 53295,248
```

The memory location 53295 corresponds to register 47 of the new VIC 8564--one of the new registers. Here you enter the same value as in the C-128 mode.

CHAPTER 14

TOKEN TABLE

BASIC commands are not stored as a character sequence in the BASIC-RAM, but turned into TOKENs. A special routine compares the entered BASIC line with commands stored in the BASIC-interpreter. If the command is found, the BASIC-interpreter gives a special character sequence instead. The bytes for RUN--82, 85, and 78--are transferred to the byte 138 ($8A).

Try entering NEW and then the line 10 RUN. Now enter the monitor and type in M1C00. You get the beginning section of the BASIC-RAM. But where is the RUN? If you look closely you'll find the value $8A in the sixth position, which is the token for RUN.

Tokens save a lot of memory for BASIC programs. Take the command for DIRECTORY. Stored character by character it would use 9 bytes. Changed into a token it only uses one.

It follows that tokens also make programs run faster. There is only one byte to compare instead of 9. The transfer does not waste any time, because the computer is in input waiting loops for most of the time you're entering BASIC program text.

The tokens start at $80 (128); this lets the computer quickly check if the characters read are BASIC commands or simply text characters. But this layout has one disadvantage--only 128 BASIC commands are available.

Many TOKENs not used on the C-64; the C-128 uses them all. But this still was not enough for the new set of BASIC 7.0. commands. The 128's programmers had a simple solution for using some TOKENs twice. They gave these TOKENs a second byte. The command BANK has the tokens $FE and $02 now. With this method you can store a lot more commands.

Now the token table:

BASIC-Command	Value (hex.)	Value (dec.)
END	$80	128
FOR	$81	129
NEXT	$82	130
DATA	$83	131
INPUT#	$84	132
INPUT	$85	133
DIM	$86	134
READ	$87	135
LET	$88	136
GOTO	$89	137
RUN	$8A	138
IF	$8B	139
RESTORE	$8C	140
GOSUB	$8D	141
RETURN	$8E	142
REM	$8F	143
STOP	$90	144
ON	$91	145
WAIT	$92	146
LOAD	$93	147
SAVE	$94	148
VERIFY	$95	149
DEF	$96	150
POKE	$97	151
PRINT#	$98	152
PRINT	$99	153
CONT	$9A	154

BASIC-Command	Value (hex.)	Value (dec.)
LIST	$9B	155
CLR	$9C	156
CMD	$9D	157
SYS	$9E	158
OPEN	$9F	159
CLOSE	$A0	160
GET	$A1	161
NEW	$A2	162
TAB (	$A3	163
TO	$A4	164
FN	$A5	165
SPC (	$A6	166
THEN	$A7	167
NOT	$A8	168
STEP	$A9	169
+	$AA	170
−	$AB	171
*	$AC	172
/	$AD	173
^	$AE	174
AND	$AF	175
OR	$B0	176
>	$B1	177
=	$B2	178
<	$B3	179
SGN	$B4	180
INT	$B5	181
ABS	$B6	182
USR	$B7	183
FRE	$B8	184
POS	$B9	185
SQR	$BA	186
RND	$BB	187
LOG	$BC	188
EXP	$BD	189
COS	$BE	190
SIN	$BF	191
TAN	$C0	192
ATN	$C1	193
PEEK	$C2	194

BASIC-Command	Value (hex.)	Value (dec.)
LEN	$C3	195
STR$	$C4	196
VAL	$C5	197
ASC	$C6	198
CHR$	$C7	199
LEFT$	$C8	200
RIGHT$	$C9	201
MID$	$CA	202
GO	$CB	203
RGR	$CC	204
RCLR	$CD	205
Two-byte token	$CE	
JOY	$CF	207
RDOT	$D0	208
DEC	$D1	209
HEX$	$D2	210
ERR$	$D3	211
INSTR	$D4	212
ELSE	$D5	213
RESUME	$D6	214
TRAP	$D7	215
TRON	$D8	216
TROFF	$D9	217
SOUND	$DA	218
VOL	$DB	219
AUTO	$DC	220
PUDEF	$DD	221
GRAPHIC	$DE	222
PAINT	$DF	223
CHAR	$E0	224
BOX	$E1	225
CIRCLE	$E2	226
GSHAPE	$E3	227
SSHAPE	$E4	228
DRAW	$E5	229
LOCATE	$E6	230
COLOR	$E7	231
SCNCLR	$E8	232
SCALE	$E9	233
HELP	$EA	234

BASIC-Command	Value (hex.)	Value (dec.)
DO	$EB	235
LOOP	$EC	236
EXIT	$ED	237
DIRECTORY	$EE	238
DSAVE	$EF	239
DLOAD	$F0	240
HEADER	$F1	241
SCRATCH	$F2	242
COLLECT	$F3	243
COPY	$F4	244
RENAME	$F5	245
BACKUP	$F6	246
DELETE	$F7	247
RENUMBER	$F8	248
KEY	$F9	249
MONITOR	$FA	250
USING	$FB	251
UNTIL	$FC	252
WHILE	$FD	253
Two-byte token	$FE	
π (Pi)	$FF	255

Next is the index for double byte TOKENs. They have two preceding
values: $CE and $FE. Index for commands with $CE as the first TOKEN:

BASIC-Command	First byte	Value (hex.)	Value (dec.)
POT	$CE	$02	2
BUMP	$CE	$03	3
PEN	$CE	$04	4
RSPPOS	$CE	$05	5
RSPRITE	$CE	$06	6
RSPCOLOR	$CE	$07	7
XOR	$CE	$08	8
RWINDOW	$CE	$09	9
POINTER	$CE	$0A	10

Index for commands with $FE as the first TOKEN:

BASIC-Command First byte Value (hex.)   Value (dec.)

===

BASIC-Command	First byte	Value (hex.)	Value (dec.)
BANK	$FE	$02	2
FILTER	$FE	$03	3
PLAY	$FE	$04	4
TEMPO	$FE	$05	5
MOVSPR	$FE	$06	6
SPRITE	$FE	$07	7
SPRCOLOR	$FE	$08	8
RREG	$FE	$09	9
ENVELOPE	$FE	$0A	10
SLEEP	$FE	$0B	11
CATALOG	$FE	$0C	12
DOPEN	$FE	$0D	13
APPEND	$FE	$0E	14
DCLOSE	$FE	$0F	15
BSAVE	$FE	$10	16
BLOAD	$FE	$11	17
RECORD	$FE	$12	18
CONCAT	$FE	$13	19
DVERIFY	$FE	$14	20
DCLEAR	$FE	$15	21
SPRSAV	$FE	$16	22
COLLISION	$FE	$17	23
BEGIN	$FE	$18	24
BEND	$FE	$19	25
WINDOW	$FE	$1A	26
BOOT	$FE	$1B	27
WIDTH	$FE	$1C	28
SPRDEF	$FE	$1D	29
QUIT	$FE	$1E	30
STASH	$FE	$1F	31
FETCH	$FE	$21	33
SWAP	$FE	$23	35
OFF	$FE	$24	36
FAST	$FE	$25	37
SLOW	$FE	$26	38

Optional Diskette

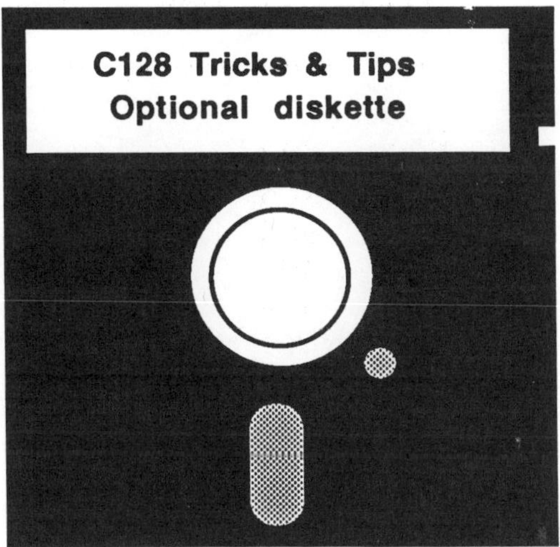

For your convenience, the program listings contained in this book are available on a 1541 formatted floppy disk. You should order the diskette if you want to use the programs, but don't want to type them in from the listings in the book.

All programs on the diskette have been fully tested. You can change the programs for your particular needs. The diskette is available for $14.95 + $2.00 ($5.00 foreign) for postage and handling.

When ordering, please give your name and shipping address. Enclose a check, money order or credit card information. Mail your order to:

Abacus Software
P.O. Box 7219
Grand Rapids, MI 49510

Or for fast service, call **616/241-5510**.

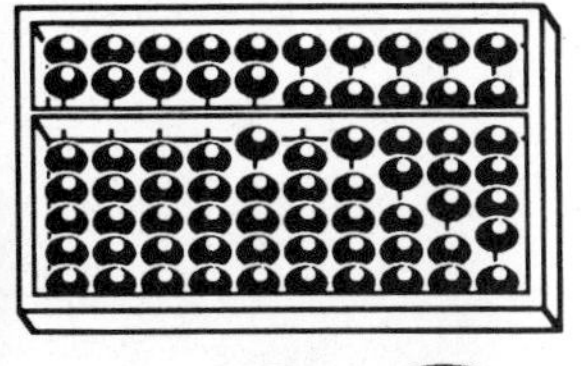

NEW '128 SOFTWARE

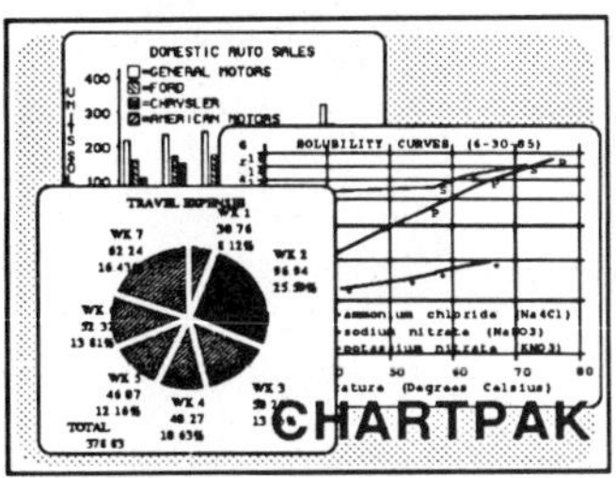

CHARTPAK
Make professional quality pie, bar and line charts, and graphics from your data. Includes statistical functions. 3x the resolution of '64 version. 500+ data points Outputs to most printers. $39.95

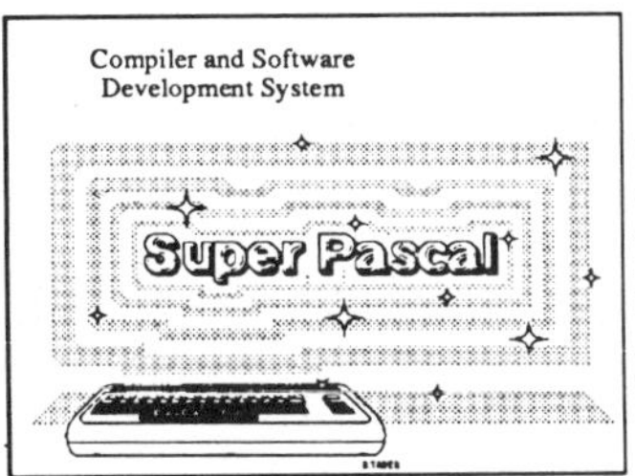

SUPER Pascal
Complete J&W development system. With enhanced editor, compiler, built-in assembler, tool-kit, graphics, 220 page handbook, and plenty more. $59.95

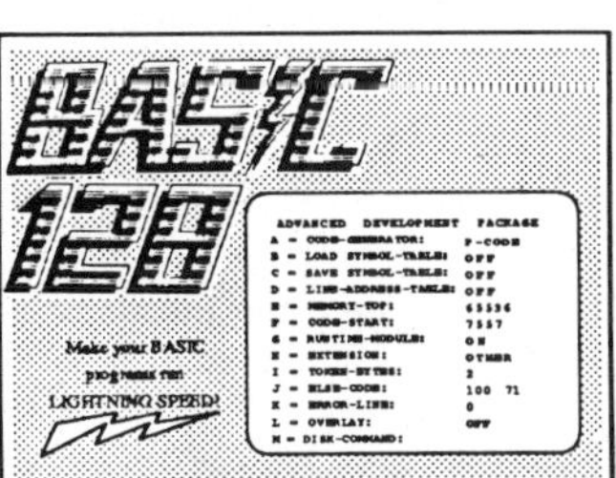

BASIC 128 Compiler
Versatile compiler instantly turns BASIC into lightning fast 6510 machine code and/or compact speedcode. Variable passing overlays, integer arithmetic, and more. $59.95

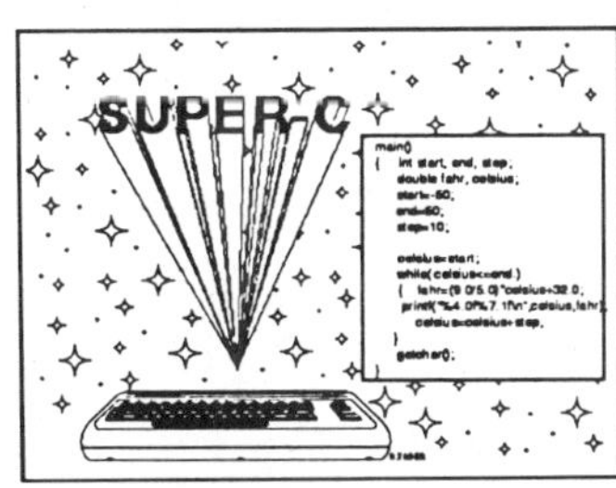

SUPER C
Complete K&R compiler and development system. Editor, compiler, linker, I/O library and extensive 200 page handbook. Creates fast 6510 machine code. $79.95

...AND OUR OTHER FANTASTIC 64 SOFTWARE

Abacus  Software

P.O. Box 7211 Grand Rapids, MI 49510 Telex 709-10 Phone 616/241-5510

Call **now** for the name of your nearest dealer. To order by credit card, MC, AMEX or VISA, call **616/241-5510**. Other software and books are available - Call and ask for your **free** catalog. Add $4.00 for shipping per order. Foreign orders add $12.00 per item. Dealer inquires welcome - 1200+ dealers nationwide.

Trusted Software and

Language Software

For Commodore Computers